CAF ICFM
THE FUNDRAISING SERIES

TRUS
FUNDRAIS

EDITOR
ANTHONY CLAY

1ST EDITION

The fundraising series
Corporate Fundraising Valerie Morton (editor)
Fundraising Strategy Redmond Mullin
Legacy Fundraising Sebastian Wilberforce (editor)

© 1999 Charities Aid Foundation and Institute of Charity Fundraising Managers

Published by:
Charities Aid Foundation
Kings Hill
West Malling
Kent
ME19 4TA

Tel +44 (0)1732 520000
Fax +44 (0)1732 520001
Web address http://www.charitynet.org
E-mail cafpubs@charitynet.org

Institute of Charity Fundraising Managers
Central Office
Market Towers
1 Nine Elms Lane
London
SW8 5NQ

Tel +44 (0)20 7627 3436
Fax +44 (0)20 7627 3508

Editor Andrew Steeds
Design and production GreenGate Publishing Services, Tonbridge
Printed and bound by Bell & Bain Ltd, Glasgow
Cover design Eugenie Dodd Typographics
A catalogue record for this book is available from the British Library
ISBN 1–85934–069–5

Contents

The fundraising series

Fundraisers have always been among the most forward thinking in their willingness to share technique and experience. It is, therefore, surprising that, while books describing successful fundraising campaigns abound, no attempt has previously been made to establish an 'accepted body of literature' explaining fundraising activity as a whole within one series of volumes.

This is precisely what **The fundraising series** seeks to do.

Each volume is complete in itself, concentrating as it does on a key element within the fundraising 'marketing mix'. Taken together, the volumes that comprise this series will provide a comprehensive survey of existing fundraising practice, identifying analysing and explaining the breadth of fundraising experience currently available.

The titles in the series are not intended as fundraising manuals but as fundraising textbooks that identify and explain accepted fundraising practice within a coherent framework that may be easily translated back to the workplace. These 'working textbooks' are to be used by academics and practitioners alike. To this end, each title addresses the core fundraising competencies contained within the Certificate of Fundraising Management qualification awarded by the ICFM.

Each title explains the historical development of the fundraising practice in question and identifies the philosophical and theoretical context within which current work practice is grounded. The main body of each text is then devoted to an analysis of current activity and the identification of key learning points to guide future action.

Without a willing cohort of fundraising specialists prepared to share their skill and experience with others, this series would simply not have been possible. My thanks to them: together they have created the first, comprehensive series of fundraising textbooks anywhere in the world.

David Ford
Chairman, ICFM

About the authors

Chris Carnie

Chris Carnie has been a fundraiser since 1980 and was a researcher in the House of Commons from 1982 to 1984. In 1990 he co-founded The Factary, Europe's only specialist prospect research agency. In 1993 he became the first fundraising researcher to be elected a Fellow of the Institute of Charity Fundraising Managers. He is Founder Chair of ICFM Researchers in Fundraising, a member of the Association of Professional Researchers for Advancement (USA), a member of the Asociación Profesional de Fundraising (Spain) and of EU Consult. Chris lives in Barcelona, Spain where he has founded Factary Europe to supply fundraisers across the continent with information, training and consultancy.

He writes and trains in fundraising research for ICFM, the British Council, Charities Aid Foundation (CAF), Prospecting for Gold, ISFG (Netherlands), the Netherlands Fundraising Handbook, the Ministerio de Asuntos Sociales (Spain) and the International Fund Raising Workshop in the Netherlands, where he is a regular Master Class leader. He is currently writing a book on fundraising and research for Directory of Social Change (DSC), London. He was featured in the Honor Roll of the Council for Advancement and Support of Education (USA) 1996–97.

Anthony Clay

After working for 10 years as Head of Fundraising at the RSPB, Anthony Clay went on to spend another 11 years working in senior consultancy, helping more than 70 charities (many of them major nationals) with strategic planning and cost-effective fundraising, especially from trusts, major gifts and legacies.

Anthony has been the trainer on the ICFM's Practitioner Course on 'Researching and Approaching Grant Making Trusts' since its inception. He has previously served as Honorary Treasurer and Chairman of the ICFM (of which he is a fellow) and is currently Chairman of the ICFM Professional Practice Committee. He is a director of FR&C Ltd, the leading Fundraising Research & Consultancy company.

Graham Collings

Graham Collings has been a fundraiser for 20 years, working with the Red Cross, British Trust for Conservation volunteers, and as a consultant with over 70 different organisations, in campaigns large and small. He currently operates as an independent fundraising consultant, providing advice, mentoring and training. He works mainly with smaller charities or difficult causes, where trusts are often the mainstay of support.

Tim Finn

Tim Finn is founder and managing director of the fundraising consultants, Collyer Finn Limited. He specialises in raising funds from the trusts sector. He works on behalf of charity clients, from the smallest to those of national size, in all parts of Britain.

Tim has contributed articles on fundraising issues to *Management Today*, Debrett's *People of Today* and several national newspapers. He also writes a regular column for *Professional Fundraising* magazine, and is an author of social histories, fiction and drama.

Peter Flory

Peter Flory is an independent information technology consultant working solely in the voluntary sector.

He has been in the IT industry for more than 30 years, spending the first 15 years in a number of technical roles and the second as a management consultant. He assists all types of non-profit-making organisations with the complete 'IT life-cycle' – from IT strategy development to requirements' specification and invitation-to-tender procedures, project management, quality assurance, implementation support and, finally, to reviews of operational systems.

Peter also runs seminars on IT strategy and on fundraising software and is a regular speaker on all manner of IT-related subjects for a variety of clients and functions.

Kay Holmes-Siedle

Kay Holmes-Siedle joined the voluntary sector twenty years ago as head of research at CAF, where she was responsible for researching and compiling what is now known as *Dimensions of the Voluntary Sector*. She also acted as Secretary to CAF's own grant-making trust.

On moving into the service sector, she joined Redmond Mullin Ltd to establish a funding and wealth database and unique press cuttings library. In the 1980s she worked closely with the NSPCC on its Centenary Campaign and helped set up the Cambridge University Development research department. Kay has spent time in the USA and Canada, as Managing Director of Chapter One's research function, observing and investigating major donor campaigns and research facilities, assimilating and bringing back the best for the UK market.

She has pioneered major donor development programmes in the UK for large national charities, including Shelter and UNICEF, and also with smaller, challenging causes. She is a director of FR&C Ltd and a Fellow of ICFM.

Adrian Longley

After almost 15 years' private practice as a solicitor, Adrian Longley spent the next 18 years of his life as legal adviser to the National Council for Voluntary Organisations, where he sat on a number of working parties, including Malpractice in Fundraising for Charity, and Effectiveness and the Voluntary Sector. In the 1970s he was a member of the Goodman Committee on Charity Law and Voluntary Organisations (which led, ultimately, to the Charities Acts of 1992 and 1993) and, more recently, a UK contributor to Les Associations en Europe – Régime Juridique et Fiscal for the Juris Service in Lyon.

An Honorary Fellow of the ICFM, Adrian is currently consultant to Arlingtons Sharmas Solicitors and, among other charities, to the Memorial Gates Trust, the Council for the Preservation of Rural England, the Russian European Trust and the Menerva Educational Trust.

Roger Mitty

Roger Mitty has been a professional fundraiser for over twenty-four years, having joined the charity Help the Aged in 1976. In 1979, he was seconded by Help the Aged to several welfare organisations in South Africa, where he set up successful fundraising operations for a number of causes, including a feeding scheme for township children and care facilities for the elderly black population in Cape Province.

In 1983, Roger was appointed head of Help the Aged's marketing group with responsibility for the charity's income from direct mail, press appeals, Adopt a Granny sponsorship, legacies, trusts and foundations, and corporate sponsorships (the income from these sources at that time was around £10 million per annum). His training in fundraising included visits to North America.

In 1986 he joined the Chapter One Group, a marketing and fundraising services company, as Client Services Director. In December 1996 he organised a management buy-out of the company, which led to the formation of FR&C Ltd, where he is currently a director, co-owner and practising consultant.

Redmond Mullin

Redmond Mullin is chairman of Redmond Mullin Ltd. Formerly a Jesuit, he has worked in research at Masius, in advertising at J Walter Thompson, in fundraising with Wells, and has been a director at CAF, where he was responsible for grant-making and grant-making policy and for production of the *Directory of Grant-Making Trusts*.

He is currently on the board of the Family Welfare Association and on the Gulbenkian's Arts, Initiatives and Money committee, and chairs the Advisory Committee for the Open University Voluntary Sector Management Programme. He has also chaired the ICFM's Fellows Working Party. As well as being a Trustee of Dartington Summer Arts Foundation, Redmond manages a significant family trust in the West Midlands and has advised Hambro Life (now Allied Dunbar) on the management, structure and policy for its grant-making trusts. He has published, lectured and broadcast extensively on fundraising and related matters.

Des Palmer

Des Palmer worked for the Allied Dunbar Charitable Trust – now the Zurich Financial Services (UKISA) Charitable Trust – from 1978 to 1996, where he was involved in a range of activities, including researching social issues, turning the findings into grant-making programmes (domestic violence, schizophrenia and dementia, to name but three), managing programmes, assessing applications and evaluating projects. He also wrote and spoke widely on fundraising for the smaller charity and on corporate community involvement.

Now a consultant to grant-making trusts, giving advice to companies and charities on evaluation, fundraising and management, Des is currently an adviser to two major grant-making trusts. He has recently published *Monitoring and Evaluation: a practical guide for grant-making trusts* and *Working Together: a practical guide to mergers and alternative options for crossroads schemes*.

David Saint

David Saint is currently director of Action Planning, which he formed in response to the demand for sound advice and practical assistance in all aspects of the voluntary sector.

Before forming Action Planning, David had spent over 20 years in charity fundraising and management, working for The Spastic's Society (as it was then called), Sense, Sane and Arthritis Care.

A regular contributor to journals, David is an associate of City University Business School and a member of the Institute of Charity Fundraising Managers. He is also an Elder and active member of his local United Reformed Church.

Nigel Siederer

Nigel Siederer has been Chief Executive of the Association of Charitable Foundations (ACF) since 1990. He has 25 years' experience in the voluntary sector, mainly with umbrella and resource organisations. The Association of Charitable Foundations has a membership of almost 300 trusts, including many of the largest: ACF member trusts give out about half of the total trust funding.

Anne Villemur

Anne Villemur retired from CAF at the end of 1995, having first joined the Foundation in 1980. She became editor of the *Directory of Grant Making Trusts* in 1982, a task in which she was greatly helped by frequent attendance at seminars and interest groups organised by the administrators of major trusts. Thanks to the insight she acquired in this way, Anne was able to set up an annual series of workshops on the theme, 'How to approach trusts'.

David Wickert

From 1992 to 1997, David Wickert was director of CAFAmerica, a 501(c) (3) non-profit with headquarters in New York.

From 1986 to 1992 he was a director of CAF in the UK, where he set up the Give As You Earn payroll deduction scheme. Prior to joining CAF, he was also the first chairman of the Waterloo Trust, chairman of the Southwark Council for Social Aid and a director of Coin Street Community Builders. He also co-founded the Upstream Theatre Club and Upstream Children's Theatre and has produced plays on London's Fringe, at the Edinburgh Festival, in the West End, on and off Broadway, as well as touring productions throughout the world.

An Anglican (Episcopalian) priest, he has been on the boards of numerous organisations and an adviser to appeals connected with the arts, housing, education and religion, both in the USA and in the UK.

He is currently chairman of the American Fund for Charities in Washington, DC and a director of Chapel & York Limited.

Foreword

Anthony Clay

This book, one in a series of fundraising titles published by ICFM/CAF, focuses on a form of fundraising that could be described as following a virtuous cycle. Grant-making trusts exist uniquely to give money away. They are also distinguished by a further set of characteristics:

- They provide highly tax-efficient methods of distributing philanthropy.
- Trustees share the decision-making process of where the money of grant-making trusts should go, whereas this may, in other organisations, be left in the hands of the philanthropist alone.
- Sometimes very experienced administrators are employed to examine projects, to carry the burden of administrative matters, to check on progress and – increasingly – to seek out new areas in need of help.
- Fundraisers are frequently able to build understanding relationships with trustees and administrators.
- Grants can sometimes be made rapidly and effectively, often at relatively short notice, where companies may need longer lead times to develop programmes of support for charities.
- Above all, grant-making trusts provide up to one-fifth of the total voluntary income of charities in this country.

For all these reasons, the benefits of grant-making trusts – in terms of relieving human suffering, encouraging the arts and protecting the environment – are enormous. However, perhaps because the cycle is so transparently virtuous, trust fundraising has not been paid the professional attention it deserves.

What information is currently available on grant-making trusts?

Many trusts (but by no means all) publish information about how much they grant, for what purpose, and what their grant-making policies are. Some also give examples of typical grants.

There have been many important publications for grant seekers and grant makers, produced by organisations like the Charities Aid Foundation (CAF) and the Directory of Social Change (DSC), which present information about trusts in directories and on CD-Rom. CAF has also published a useful book on *Applying to a Grant Making Trust* in its 'How to' series (Villemur, 1996).

The Institute of Charity Fundraising Managers (ICFM) has prepared helpful handouts on the subject for its regular practitioner course on the subject, and the DSC has also prepared course material.

Other organisations provide search facilities to enable fundraisers to focus on those that are likely to be of most relevance to their causes (see 'Useful publications and sources of information' at the end of this book). Fundraising research companies identify suitable trusts for their charity clients, sometimes using inside information that greatly supplements the information in the published material. Fundraising consultants will assist the development of strategies for researching and approaching trusts. Several organisations provide training for fundraisers and volunteers on how to tap into this important source of income.

Yet this book is the first attempt to produce a publication that brings all these elements together in one volume, written by a range of contributors selected for their knowledge, experience and skills in each aspect of the subject.

The audience and the aims of this book

This book will be of value and interest to all who seek money from grant-making trusts, including private individuals, but the main audiences are trustees and employees of charities of all sizes. It is not, strictly speaking, a 'text book'; it is more of a compendium of the opinion and experience of a wide range of experienced authors. For those seeking a major treatise on the law relating to charitable trusts, Adrian Longley's chapter on 'The nature and structure of grant-making trusts in the UK' in this book is an excellent introduction, but there is much more to be read elsewhere. Those contemplating huge multi-million pound appeals should seek out several books available on how to win major gift campaigns, of which trust fundraising simply forms a part.

Fundraising has never been more competitive than now: the number of grant-seeking charities grows each year; state support for existing charities is declining; the demand for lottery-grant partnership funding continues unabated; many organisations that used not to be charities, such as NHS hospitals, are now hard at work seeking voluntary income. A book like this, which brings together the collective wisdom of so many experienced people, is timely indeed.

Much has been done (by organisations such as the Association of Grant Making Trusts, the training courses of the ICFM and others) to raise standards of application and grant making. Regrettably, however, there are far too many badly presented requests directed at overloaded trustees, seeking grants for irrelevant projects from trusts that are already fully committed.

The aim of this book is to help to ensure that more of the right applications reach the right trusts, at the right time, for the right sums of money, for the right projects. This is no mean task for a single publication, but if it achieves a small part of those objectives it is to be hoped that all of its many contributors will feel that their efforts have been worthwhile.

The structure of this book

Part 1 of this book provides an overview of grant-making trusts in terms of their history and structure: Anne Villemur writes a brief history of trusts; Adrian Longley presents the nature and structure of modern grant-making trusts from the legal point of view, setting the framework in which they must operate; Chris Carnie outlines the size of the sector and its relative importance in a fundraising strategy.

Part 2 concentrates on the importance of research in trust fundraising: Kay Holmes-Siedle writes on where to look and how to go about researching appropriate trusts; Redmond Mullin describes how to assemble a charity's funding needs into a coherent series of projects for support; Graham Collings completes this part of the book by addressing the question of how to plan each trust approach strategy.

Part 3 is given over to approaching grant-making trusts and considers the formal application, leaning on the practical advice provided by grant makers: Tim Finn describes how to make proper contact with each trust without breaking the rules, and Anthony Clay writes on making the application; completing this part of the book, Des Palmer, formerly a trust administrator, presents the grant maker's perspective, giving advice to grant seekers on what, and what not, to do.

In Part 4, David Saint deals with acknowledgement, recognition, reporting and keeping the trusts interested and involved. Roger Mitty follows this with a description of the process of consolidating what has been achieved, while Peter Flory writes on the computer systems needed, what can go wrong with them and how to avoid problems while creating an invaluable tool for the future.

Part 5 addresses some additional perspectives: Nigel Siederer of the Association of Charitable Foundations (ACF) sets out the views of many of the major funders; David Wickert provides a chapter on USA Foundations, some of which may be highly relevant to UK charities.

The final chapters in the book conclude the contributions, provide information about useful publications and organisations and give a glossary of terms to complete the picture.

Acknowledgements

This is a wide source of information. Inevitably, not all our contributors agree on all aspects of the subject, but all that has been written reflects experienced and practical observations of what has worked in the past, even if it may not necessarily work in the future.

I am deeply grateful to all these contributors and also, for inviting me to act as editor and for their great help and guidance throughout the project, to David Moncrieff of CAF and to Stephen Lee, formerly Director of ICFM. I am especially grateful to the Association of Grant Making Trusts for permission to use their excellent advice material and to numerous trust administrators who have commented on the work and responded to my frequent cries for help. Nor must I forget the charity clients of mine who have allowed me to help them with their trust fundraising and have, in return, allowed me to learn practically all I know about the subject.

There are many others who deserve unreserved thanks, not least all the philanthropists who have so thoughtfully and generously set aside their wealth for the sake of others, and the innumerable trustees who give freely of their time to lead the trusts and award the grants. My very special personal thanks go to my friends and fellow directors at FR&C Ltd, Kay Homes-Siedle and Roger Mitty, who have lent their fullest support to the project and have, indeed, contributed two key chapters to it.

Finally, I must thank Linda Payne for the huge task of typing from so many varying manuscripts but, above all, my dear wife, Liz, who has for 34 years borne my late hours in the office with unfailing fortitude.

Introduction

Anthony Clay

What do we mean by trusts?

In the United States charities are divided into two groups: *public charities* have multiple sources of income and exist mainly to carry out charitable work themselves; *foundations* are usually funded by one or, at most, a few benefactors and exist to give money away to good causes. Different rules apply to these two types of charitable organisation. Specifically, foundations are required by US law not only to distribute their income but also to give away 5 per cent of their capital fund each year.

No such precise definitions or legal requirements about distributing capital apply in this country. All registered charities are treated in much the same way, whether they be grant receiving, grant making, or both.

The words we use

The words 'trust' and 'foundation' are virtually synonymous, and other words like 'settlement' or 'charity' are in common use. All charitable foundations are trusts, that is they are managed by trustees who may, or may not, be supported by paid staff. A 'foundation' is a trust whose income is derived from an endowment of land or invested capital. Not all foundations make grants; some use their income to finance charitable work of their own.

This book is not primarily concerned with charitable trusts such as those major national organisations that carry out their own programmes of work. Nor is it concerned with those (such as the World Wide Fund for Nature or the Cancer Research Fund) that, although carrying out few projects of their own, exist primarily to give money proactively to relevant projects of their own choosing. This book is concerned principally with trusts that have been set up by their founders as vehicles for the distribution of philanthropy, either for general charitable purposes or for the benefit of specific causes or groups of causes. Such trusts tend to fall into one of the following five groupings.

'Institutional' trusts

These are trusts that were set up several years ago with a number of trustees, like the Wellcome Foundation. They make grants according to very detailed procedures, making use of relevant professionals. Usually grant decisions are made at peer level, so, typically, scientists present proposals for approval by other scientists.

'Private' trusts

Private trusts are set up by one individual who takes most of the grant-making decisions on their own or in discussion with a spouse. Such trusts are often primarily set up for reasons of tax efficiency.

'Family' trusts

These trusts are often set up by one individual, often in memory of an earlier family member or as a result of a discretionary form of will, with trustees who are usually related, or at least closely connected to each other. Decisions tend to be taken collectively but informally.

'Corporate' trusts

Corporate trusts are where the income of the trust (and therefore its ability to make grants) is dependent upon the profits of a company or a group of companies. Decisions tend to be made by committees, ratified by directors of the company: these trusts now increasingly take account of employees' views and interests.

'Combination' trusts

These trusts are essentially a combination of one or more of the above groupings.

Such categorisation, though helpful in explaining the nature of the sector, can be misleading: few trusts fit neatly into one group, and trusts sometimes change from one group to another. Nevertheless, as will be seen later in this book, understanding the structures, decision-making procedures, objectives and policies of each trust to which you apply is absolutely fundamental to successful trust fundraising.

Unfortunately, these important distinctions are rarely appreciated by grant seekers. Application is too often seen as a simple process requiring only casual research of published directories, followed by mass mailing of word-processed request letters.

An important revenue source

There are well over 8,500 grant-making trusts in the UK, making grants totalling over £1,500 million a year. This is much more than the total of local authority contributions to the voluntary sector. Chris Carnie (see Chapter 3) estimates that 15–20 per cent of the income of fundraising organisations comes from such trusts. So grant-making trusts are a very important revenue source indeed.

Trusts have great advantages as sources of income for charities:

- They exist to give money away. Other sources, such as companies and individuals, do not.
- Grant-making decision makers are often looking for new ideas and new directions. The modern pattern is for them to be seeking continually to be moving forward, so that past grant receivers do not become dependant on them.
- Towards the end of each of their financial years many trusts find themselves with money left over from previous allocations to projects that did not proceed.
- Most trust administrators are very experienced and keen to help charities to apply. The days when some administrators seemed to exist simply to say 'no' are largely past.

The place of trust fundraising in a charity's fundraising strategy

Trust fundraising should not stand alone as a fundraising method. Essentially it should be part of an overall strategic plan, a key part of an overall approach in which the wider interests of the need to meet all of a charity's objectives are paramount. Sometimes this may mean holding back on a trust-fundraising programme in order to prevent a relatively low-level application from preceding a much larger request.

A serious problem can arise when a charity is fundraising 'in boxes'. Typically, the fundraising department of a middle-sized or major charity will have a number of sections. These sections might include a corporate unit, a legacy unit, a special-events unit and a trust unit, each of which will have its own budgets, targets or goals to achieve. A structure of this kind can lead to each unit's becoming too possessive of its sectional interests. Ways have to be found to ensure that jealousies and self-interests do not get in the way of more important matters.

Who should we listen to: the fundraiser or the grant maker?

The duty of grant makers is to ensure that, as cost effectively as possible, the money they have to give away goes to the best projects that are most relevant to the trust's objectives and the trustees' policies and priorities.

The duty of fundraisers is to secure as much money as possible for their cause, with complete honesty, while complying with the requirements of the law and following best practice.

The difference between the two is epitomised by the different answers given to the question: 'Should fundraisers go straight to the grant maker's trustees, or to the administrator, grant secretary or correspondent?'

The Association of Grant Making Trusts advises quite clearly that the approach should be to the administrators, who are appointed by the trustees for the very purpose of protecting them from the thousands of applications that are made each week.

The experienced fundraiser will say that it is crucial to seek to make contact with the trustees whenever possible. It is the trustees who make the final decisions, and there is a duty on fundraisers to go to the top – to the people who matter most. Of course, when making formal applications, the routes the grant maker lays down should be followed. But imagine how more successful it would be if, at the vital moment of decision making, a request is fully understood and endorsed by the majority of the trustees who know the project and some of the people involved in it. Often it is much easier for trustees to say 'no' to people they do not know than to people they do.

Unashamedly, this book sides with the fundraisers on this issue in the hope that, when each side understands the other, the virtuous cycle occurs where trusts make major contributions to pioneering projects that make a significant difference to the fulfilment of important charitable objectives.

PART **ONE**

Grant-making trusts

CHAPTER ONE

The historical context

Anne Villemur

Introduction

Unlike any other source of funding for charitable work (eg the general public, corporate and statutory bodies), a grant-making trust is set up for the sole purpose of grant-aiding charities, voluntary organisations and individuals to help advance their work. When a trust is set up in England and Wales, a Trust Deed is drawn up and registered at the Charity Commission, setting out its aims and objectives and listing the founding trustees. As a registered charitable body, the new trust's income will be exempt from any tax. The trustees are in sole charge of the distribution of grants provided, of course, that the grants be made for charitable purposes as expressed within the trust deed of the trust.

A brief history of grant-making trusts

Grant-making trusts are not entirely an invention of the twentieth century. Of the 2,500 or so trusts listed in CAF's *Directory of Grant Making Trusts*, 109 were set up before 1900. Where did the idea stem from? On what base were the trusts built?

The financial underpinning of the earlier trusts was to be found in the following four main areas.

Religious and church property

These trusts range from the very large, such as the City Parochial Foundation, to a myriad of very small parochial funds, many of which have remained hidden for decades. Efforts have been made in various parts of the country to uncover these hidden pools of wealth.

Property (for example, land)

The oldest and largest of these, founded in 1626, is the Henry Smith's Charity, of which the assets include large swathes of Kensington.

Livery companies

The area of benefit of such trusts is often very limited. The Cripplegate Foundation, established in 1891, is restricted to The Ancient Parish of St Giles, Cripplegate (ie Southern Islington and the North of the City of London).

Bequests

Nowadays, charitable bequests contained in wills are likely to leave money to a named charity, because so many of the larger charities have gained the status of household names. In previous times, bequests tended to be made in perpetuity for specific purposes in a small geographical area. One example of the more unusual purposes was money left to 'provide red flannel once a year to the poorer children in the village'.

Judged by the amount of money they give away, trusts established before 1900 are relatively unimportant, accounting for only approximately 7 per cent of the total grants of all trusts listed in the *Directory of Grant Making Trusts*.

Trusts in the twentieth century

Many important trusts were established in the early part of this century, often motivated by religion. People who had built up large fortunes through successful commercial ventures felt that it was only right to share some of their wealth with the less fortunate. Quaker families, in particular, set up a number of important trusts. Such a sense of social conscience was not always the motivating factor, however: one large trust was created because the family of the Settlor wanted to avoid swingeing 'death duties'.

A table contained in a recent edition of the *Directory of Grant Making Trusts* shows that from 1950 onwards the number of trusts set up per year increased dramatically, with by far the largest group of trusts being established between 1961 and 1980. One of the reasons for this is that charities and charitable trusts had come under scrutiny: in 1952, the Nathan Committee on Charitable Trusts reported that, for trusts to be of maximum benefit to the community, it was essential to produce a means by which trusts could learn of each other's existence. This means came into being with the Charities Act 1960 which, among other things, established a Central Register of Charities open to the public. Heightened public awareness of charity in general and of the relationship of charitable trusts to charitable activity may have resulted in philanthropically minded persons deciding to establish charitable trusts rather than make straight donations to the charities of their choice.

Inevitably, this increased knowledge exposed the trusts to a publicity their trustees would gladly have avoided. Not only were they exposed to public view on the Central Register at the Charity Commission in London but, in 1968, the first edition of the *Directory of Grant Making Trusts* was published.

At the time, most trustees felt that their trust was a private, family affair and that they were quite capable of deciding to whom grants should go. The concept of a partnership between grant-makers and grant-seekers was something only envisaged by the more radically minded trusts.

Into the limelight

The first publication of the *Directory of Grant Making Trusts* in 1968 represents a turning point. Shortly after publication, the publishers began to be the target of angry letters from trusts accusing them of causing a 'bombardment of applications' with which they could not cope. The privacy of trusts had been threatened, and they were not impressed by the argument that, because their incomes were tax free, their decisions should be subject to public scrutiny. Some insisted that for subsequent editions their entries should include the admonition, 'No unsolicited applications will be considered by the trustees'.

This negative reaction may have had something to do with the fact that the average board of trustees at that time was middle-aged and middle class: even the salaried directors of the larger trusts were drawn from the ranks of the retired professional classes.

The American context

On the international scene, it is in the USA that trusts and foundations have become most common. As may be expected from the fact that a great number of these trusts and foundations are based in commercial companies, they are extremely business-like. In the past, American foundations associated with each other in a way that could not have been envisaged by their UK counterparts at the time. Currently, their professional association, based at the Foundation Center in New York, has a large staff headed by a President who played an important role in the life of US Foundations. The Center publishes a comprehensive Directory of Foundations, plus a Register setting out details of actual grants made. It also provides help to grant-seeking bodies in the shape of workshops on how best to prepare an application (or 'proposal' as they are called in the USA).

Some say good ideas take a certain time to cross the Atlantic from west to east. Little by little, UK trusts began to get together to discuss their grant making. At first, this was an 'old boys' network' of directors of major trusts, but, once the first step away from anonymity had been taken (with the Charities Act and the publication of the *Directory of Grant Making Trusts*), things were bound to change. Trusts began to employ more and more paid staff, and assistant directors formed a loose association that met at residential seminars to which experts in the sociological field were invited to address delegates from a wide variety of trusts.

Another idea to have made the same journey is that of the community foundation: there are now 24 established community trusts and foundations in the UK and a similar number of emerging foundations, all supported by the Association of Community Trusts and Foundations (ACTAF).

The current position

A new type of trust director began to emerge in the late 1980s. Many had a background of social work that made them naturally inclined to share information and opinions about the work their trustees were likely to find. There is now in the UK an Association of Charitable Foundations (ACF) (founded in 1989), which gathers together a number of important trusts. ACF organises highly successful conferences and seminars and serves as a base for the meetings of various interest groups that study specific problems. It also comments on all aspects of grant-making procedure in its quarterly magazine *Trust and Foundation News*.

This new togetherness sends a very positive signal to most grant-seekers who, in the past, felt that the relationship between them and grant makers was very much 'them and us'. Some fundraisers remain sceptical, and one of them is reported to have said: ' Applying to trusts is a game – and more like snakes and ladders than like chess.'

CHAPTER TWO

The nature and structure of grant-making trusts in the UK

Adrian Longley

Things and actions are what they are and the consequences of them will be what they will be; why then should we desire to be deceived?
Bishop Butler (1692–1752) *Fifteen Sermons*, No 7

The trustees, who admitted to a lapse of judgement over the margarine, have suspended further endorsements until they draw up rules on what products are suitable. They have rejected requests for a Diana manure and rose-coloured carpets with her signature.
The Times, 25 April 1998

Introduction

Even if the trustees of the Diana, Princess of Wales Memorial Fund had weighed – or had weighed more carefully – Bishop Butler's famous admonition (contained, incidentally, in a sermon on the Old Testament prophet, Balaam, whose ass, it will be recalled, was more perceptive than her master), there is, of course, no guarantee that they would have acted otherwise and so escaped serious criticism and loss of public confidence. What their confessed miscalculation indisputably illustrates is that in grant-making trusts (more than in just about any other area of philanthropic endeavour) those involved in management and administration, either actually or prospectively, must never deceive themselves about the potential consequences of their actions, or their lack of actions.

A grant-making trust is often set up as a charity – by reason of the perceived fiscal and other privileges that charities enjoy – but it need not always be one; indeed, there can be circumstances where charity status is not in the best financial interests of the potential beneficiaries. Moreover, since charities are subject to constraints, including a supervisory regime maintained by the

Charity Commissioners, promoters must from the outset be clear as to the permitted scope, direction and development of their intended activities. In particular, they must fully comprehend the nature (and limitations) of charity status, the duties and responsibilities of trustees, the constitutional forms available, the procedures for establishment and dissolution and, especially in this context, certain basic principles underlying trustees' policy decisions. Each of these important elements will now be considered in turn.

Charity status

The legal and the Biblical (or popular) meanings of charity are by no means the same, though they may coincide. 'Charity' may still primarily suggest concern for those in need, hardship or distress, but in practice the range of activities recognised as charitable *by the law* is extremely wide. Moreover, as Lord Hailsham emphasised in the House of Lords in 1980, 'the legal conception of charity [is] not static, but moving and changing'.

There is no neat, encapsulated definition of a charity. The Charities Act 1993 – the latest legislation in this field – repeats an earlier Act of 1960 when it in effect describes a charity as an institution established for 'charitable purposes'. These charitable purposes are nowhere defined in statute, but their origin is, paradoxically, an Act of Parliament of 1601 (two years before the death of Elizabeth 1) or rather its preamble or introduction, which lists various activities considered charitable in Tudor times.

The 1601 Act has long been repealed, but from the beginning of the seventeenth century to the present day the courts have used the list in the preamble as a means of determining what is or is not charitable in law.

At each end of the nineteenth century, an eminent judge produced a useful classification (not a definition) of what constitutes a charity at law. Lord MacNaghten's familiar four heads of 1891 are:

- the relief of poverty;
- the advancement of education;
- the advancement of religion;
- some other purposes beneficial to the community.

With the exception of the relief of poverty, there must always be benefit to the public or to a sufficient section of the public.

Unless the promoters of a grant-making trust have a restricted category of beneficiaries in mind (for example, the needy in a particular part of the world), it is generally prudent to declare comprehensive objects along the following lines: 'To promote such objects as are now or may hereafter be deemed by law to be charitable.'

In this way, there will be no limit to the kind of charitable beneficiaries who may legitimately be supported.

Sometimes, however, any charitable objects may in practice be inappropriate. For example, where considerable sums of money have been raised from a generous public in response to a disaster appeal, the trustees of a trust established as a charity may well be precluded by the law from providing help that goes beyond the relief of genuine and immediate need. Any material enhancement of the victims' or their dependants' previous living standards can thus be unlawful. This would present the trustees with problems over the distribution of surplus funds in their hands, unless the point has been specifically covered in the appeal and/or the constitution. (The trustees of a non-charitable grant-making trust are also far less likely than those of a charity to be embarrassed by endorsements of margarine, manure, matting or any other commercial products.)

There is, of course, a crucial distinction between the objects of a charity and the means of achieving them. The former must be exclusively charitable in the strict legal sense; the latter need not – indeed, by definition, cannot – be since they will include what are essentially commercial operations, from employing staff, providing pensions and investing funds to effecting insurance cover and acquiring and disposing of property. Clearly, in the case of a grant-making trust, the trustees' investment powers should be as wide as the law permits; where substantial shareholdings are envisaged, for example, the constitution should specifically allow legal ownership by a nominee company, along with reporting procedures and all necessary safeguards for the trustees (who remain ultimately personally accountable). As far as insurance is concerned, charity trustees may not lawfully pay the premiums for a policy protecting them from the consequences of reckless breach of trust or breach of duty. However, they may in certain circumstances, and when authorised by their constitution or the Charity Commissioners, meet the cost of indemnity cover for acts properly undertaken in the course of administration, or in breach of trust, but under an honest mistake – or the costs of successfully defending a criminal prosecution brought against them in their capacity of trustees. In any event, whatever is done by or on behalf of a charity must always be in furtherance of its declared charitable objects.

Unless specifically exempt or excepted by regulations, a charity should be registered with the Charity Commissioners. Registration neither confers charity status nor is an indication that the Commissioners approve or disapprove of a charity's activities – or even that they are satisfied that it has been or will be well managed. It is, however, proof for all practical purposes that the organisation is a charity at law; and some potential donors are explicitly prevented by their own terms of reference from supporting bodies that are not registered charities.

The duties and responsibilities of trustees

Trustees are persons who hold property that they are legally bound to apply in all respects for the benefit of others.

Charity trustees are defined in section 97 of the Charities Act 1993 as 'the persons having the general conduct and management of the administration of a charity'. They are neither required nor expected by the law to be omniscient. However, they must at all times act rationally, sensibly and carefully; they must take as much care in their business dealings on behalf of their charity as would prudent men and women over their own personal business matters. Not least, they must never allow their own personal views or prejudices to influence their conduct as trustees. Yet, *On Trust*, the 1992 report of a working party on trustee training, set up by the National Council for Voluntary Organisations (NCVO) and the Charity Commission, revealed that of those surveyed only one-third actually realised they were charity trustees with strict obligations in law. Some charitable governing instruments (for example those in the form of an incorporated association) never mention the words 'trustee' or 'trustees', which may help to explain, if not wholly to excuse, the prevailing ignorance.

Trustees must, in the words of a 1990 NCVO report, *Effectiveness and the Voluntary Sector*:

> supervise the charity's operations and ensure that the strategic planning which guides those operations makes the best use of its actual and potential assets in meeting its defined aims. They are responsible for setting the targets, standards and working methods of the organisation and for being ready to modify these to meet changing circumstances.

Collectively and individually, charity trustees are responsible for all their charity's activities. Unlike private trustees, they do not need to be unanimous, but a dissenting minority will not escape responsibility unless they actively and publicly dissociate themselves from the relevant decision. Nor can the trustees, as a body, avoid ultimate responsibility by delegation to employees, agents or volunteers. However, a trustee who has acted prudently and within the scope of the charity's constitution will usually have the right to be indemnified out of the charity's assets. On the other hand, where a trustee's conduct has been negligent, reckless or outside the scope of the constitution, no indemnity will be allowed.

Constitutional form

Of the three forms realistically available, the promoters of a charitable grant-making trust in practice have to choose between a declaration of trust and incorporation as a company limited by guarantee. The structure of an unincorporated association, which frequently involves a membership wielding ultimate authority in general meeting, is not normally to be recommended in this context. Nor should a decision to incorporate be taken lightly since it will inevitably involve not only compliance with both company and charity law but also additional expense and a degree of sophistication on the part of the promoters.

Incorporation is widely seen as providing blanket limitation of trustees' personal liability, but this is a dangerous misconception. Incorporation may well afford the directors of a charitable company some initial protection against liability to the suppliers of goods and services. However, in practice, so far as ultimate personal liability is concerned, there may be little or no material difference between, on the one hand, the position of the trustees of an unincorporated association or a declaration of trust and, on the other, that of the directors of a charitable company. Undeniably, incorporation has attractions where the charity is likely to handle large sums of money and employ staff on a significant scale. But, in the case of relatively small organisations, the bureaucratic requirements can outweigh the advantages.

On balance, a declaration of trust, which is relatively easy to establish and for which there are a number of useful precedents (acceptable to the Charity Commissioners), may often be the most appropriate in this context. The trustees of such trusts are almost always a self-appointed, self-perpetuating oligarchy not accountable to a participating membership.

Formation and dissolution

If a trust has decided against charity status at the outset, no particular problems normally arise, beyond ensuring that the constitution correctly expresses the promoters' aspirations and lays down appropriate rules for management and administration – all within the general law. A special procedure, however, applies in the case of charities.

Until very recently, the recommendation was that the Charity Commission cleared a draft constitution before the formalities were completed. Today, promoters must first obtain a copy of the Commission's registration information pack, 'Starting a Charity and Applying for Registration', unless circumstances are exceptional (for example when delay in formation could result in the loss of a substantial sum of money and the Commission is therefore willing to approve a *draft* accompanied by supporting information). This information pack contains a set of documents designed to answer fundamental questions about charities, their formation and administration. The promoters must then carry through the necessary formalities: preparing, executing (and, where necessary, stamping) the constitution; completing a detailed application form (and questionnaire) for registration; signing a declaration to the effect that they have read certain of the Commission's leaflets and information sheets and understand the responsibilities of charity trustees.

Policy

All trusts are different: individual interests and styles depend on the trusts' histories, their policies and priorities – and, of course, the personalities and preferences of the trustees at any given time.

However, there are certain elements of principle and practice that the trustees of all grant-making trusts should constantly observe:

- Although the trustees must bear in mind the trust's origin and ethos, they must not be impervious to organic change in the light of shifting social, economic and political conditions.
- A primary duty of the trustees under the law is to secure the best financial return on their investments. However, in certain circumstances ethical considerations may have to be taken into account – and a lower return accepted. For example, where a trust's declared object or principal activity in practice is the relief of sufferers from cancer or even the protection of health generally, the trustees must be extremely cautious over investing in a company promoting tobacco sales (not always easy to avoid in these days of conglomerates).
- The trustees must decide on the kinds of grants they are normally prepared to make and whether they will invite applications or find other methods of identifying potential beneficiaries.
- When applications are numerous, the trustees will need to reduce these to manageable proportions, perhaps by dividing the task of detailed consideration between various members of the trustee body.
- It is often wise to check on an applicant's other sources of funds or income (including the effects that assistance from the trust may have on statutory or other benefits). In some cases, grants by instalments and/or on conditions may be sensible for both donor and donee.
- Monitoring of the actual use of funds should be through regular questionnaires and, where feasible, unannounced spot-checks. At the same time the trustees should endeavour to limit expenses to what is essential to keep the administrative wheels in motion. This, of course, is largely a matter of judgement for each trustee body.

Trustees of grant-making trusts are not governmental bodies disbursing taxpayers' money under statutory or other controls. Within the terms of their trust – and bearing in mind the warnings given in their very different ways by

Bishop Butler in the eighteenth century and the Trustees of the Diana, Princess of Wales Memorial Fund in the twentieth – they have the capacity to be pragmatic, open-minded, imaginative, even unorthodox and, above all, independent. In the end, intuition and experience often come to be the most critical components in any of their managerial or grant-making decisions.

CHAPTER **THREE**

Trusts as a fundraising source

Chris Carnie

Introduction

As you will discover from the rest of this book, the word 'trust' causes wild confusion among people inside and outside the fundraising world. The matter is not helped, frankly, by adding the commonly used 'grant-making' in front of the 'trust'. To take one, hypothetical, example, Susie, Head of Fundraising at the Fight Cancer Fund, considers the Esmee Fairbairn Charitable Trust to be a grant-making trust. To her, the Imperial Cancer Research Fund (ICRF) is clearly a fundraising competitor. As far as David, Professor of Oncology at Rutland University, is concerned, ICRF is a grant maker that supports his research lab with generous donations each year. So is Esmee Fairbairn.

To avoid this confusion this chapter will focus on organisations whose remit is primarily philanthropic – who give but who don't actively fundraise. These entities will be called simply 'trusts'.

Size of the sector – and a nationalist's warning

Including all trusts as defined above, Pharoah and Siederer (CAF, 1997) estimate there are 8,793 trusts in the UK making grants totalling £1.53 billion. This is substantially more than the total income to the voluntary sector from local authorities, valued at £1.25 billion per annum in 1997.

According to another source (Rattigan, 1997), the top 3,000 charities had a total income of £11.7 billion. This group, which confusingly includes grant-makers and fundraisers, represents most charity activity in the UK, so trust funds could be estimated as representing 13 per cent of the money flowing into the sector. This statistic will strike many as an underestimate; many would have expected that around 15–20 per cent of the income of fundraising organisations would come from trusts.

Unfortunately, as is so often the case in the voluntary sector, it is impossible to unpick the statistics to arrive at the truth. As a broad measure, however, for each £5–£8 raised in the UK, £1 comes from trusts.

Data from Scotland has been much harder to come by, and that from Northern Ireland almost impossible. So the term 'UK' should be read with caution.

The big ones

The trust world is dominated by big organisations. The two largest – the National Lottery Charities Board and the Wellcome Trust – account together for just over 35 per cent of trust grants in the UK by value. Ranking trusts by size, the yawning gap between these two giants (giving away £320 million and £219 million respectively) and the rest of the field – starting with the Garfield Weston Foundation at a mere £24 million – is evident.

In fact, the world of trusts divides neatly into three groups. The first group, representing £45 in every £100 of all grants made, includes the two giants and nine other large trusts, each of which give away more than £10 million per annum. This elite group gives away in total £692.3 million per annum.

The second group is much more numerous, but financially less important. This group contains the 1,753 trusts that make grants between £10,000 and £9.9 million. The typical grant maker in this group has an income of £55,338 per annum, makes grants of £44,076 and has assets of £537,788. This group represents 30 per cent of all grants made by value and is the place where most fundraisers expend most effort – often for small returns.

The third group – 'the rest' – is a hodge-podge of trusts which includes: around 7,000 trusts that give less than £10,000 per annum; local trusts; trusts that don't appear in the main directories; trusts about which not enough is yet known. This group represents 27 per cent of all grant pounds and is the place where many of us believe there is scope for more effective fundraising.

Numbers

Pharoah and Siederer (1997) put the total number of grant-making trusts in the UK, excluding the fundraising charities that also make grants (such as Imperial Cancer Research Fund) at 8,780. This figure is calculated by reviewing the guides produced by the two main publishers in England – CAF and the DSC.

As noted, neither of these publishers has much on Scotland, and they have even less on Northern Ireland. The Scottish Council for Voluntary Organisations (SCVO) has published a Directory including 550 grant-making trusts that responded to a questionnaire. SCVO sent the questionnaire to 22,000 charitable organisations and had just 2,500 responses in total; on that basis one could guess that there may be in Scotland 1,000–2,000 grant-making trusts, the vast majority of which will not be included in Pharoah and Siederer's count. If trusts based in Northern Ireland are taken into account, the true UK total may be between 10,000 and 11,000.

Trustees' selection policies

For fundraisers, trusts fall into two categories: those in which the trustees, or more commonly one trustee, select the grant recipients; those that have a secretariat that makes the selections.

The latter are sometimes called 'application-driven' trusts – meaning that they have an established paper procedure for grant seekers. Fill in the form, meet the criteria, and, with luck, you're in the money. Some trusts can be more mechanistic than others. One major trust looks for key words in applications: if 'women' and 'poverty' are not included, then forget it. Another uses 'poverty postcodes' to select projects: if your project is in BS2, then you pass; it it's BS8, you fail.

These systems were designed to promote equality of opportunity among grant-seekers and help to ensure that there can be no hint of patronage about trust giving. Unfortunately they sometimes have the reverse effect, where the largest, most powerful charities employ consultants who know the selection criteria (in some cases the very consultants who wrote the criteria) to boost their chances.

Most trusts are not 'application driven'. In these cases, a group of trustees meet to discuss applications received and to select this month's/year's/quarter's batch of recipients. These boards of trustees can consist simply of a wealthy trust founder and their lawyer, a group of friends, or an accountant or lawyer acting on the wishes of the (late) trust founder. As a fundraiser, this last group can be the trickiest to work with – too busy to really consider applicants, and too cautious to do anything other than interpret the founder's trust deed to the letter, their giving practices are often deeply conservative.

These groups all have one feature in common. They are human beings affected, like the rest of us, by today's earthquake or tomorrow's poor, sick child. Their giving reflects these trends, and it is artificial, in these 'non-application' trusts, to distinguish between giving by trusts and giving by the public in general.

The same methods of fundraising work for these trusts as for the rest of the populace: direct personal requests work best. If that means one person talking to another, so much the better.

SWOT of grant-making trusts as a fundraising source

What are the pros and cons of using trusts as a key fundraising source?

STRENGTHS

- The availability of information: there are directories on UK trusts from at least four major publishers (CAF, DSC, CaritasData, K G Saur) and on Scottish trusts from two (DSC and SCVO). So it's easy to find basic information on trusts.
- Trusts seem to like to fund over a period, typically, of three years. This means stability and the potential for planning.
- Trusts only exist to give money away.

WEAKNESSES

- Conversely (see Strengths) there is a lack of researched information on trusts – especially as it relates to attitudes among trustees.
- Poor-quality administration and classification by the Charity Commission for England and Wales. When asked recently to produce a list of grant-making trusts that would support mental health, the Commission was able, from 180,000 records, to produce just one. It was a hospital.
- Lack of public access to trust information in Scotland (where the Inland Revenue has imposed the sort of secrecy normally used in Liechtenstein to ensure that fundraisers can't get their hands on trust financial or management information. In what sense, one wonders, are these funds held 'on trust'?). The same applies in Northern Ireland, where the best efforts of fundraising researchers have led to an anonymous Stormont official declaring that absolutely no information is available.

OPPORTUNITIES

- A cadre of professional trust managers is developing, and with it systems for managing the selection of grant recipients. It is becoming more possible, with larger trusts, to predict where the money will go. That means better targeting, reducing waste and cost.
- Trusts outside the UK. In most countries of the world with any sort of market economy there are grant-making trusts – normally called foundations. UK fundraisers are only now beginning to understand the potential of this huge market in India, Germany, France and, of course, the USA. CAF, as part of a network of European foundations, has an agreement on transferring funds tax-efficiently across borders from and to any country in Europe.

Recently a CAF insider told me that, to date, no one has used the system.

- There is a large pool of local trusts, not contained in the standard directories.

- Administrative overload – too many trusts are drowning in inappropriate applications.
- Diminishing numbers of newly created trusts – the result, anecdotally, of two factors: first, that rich people have learned that to create a trust is to put your head above the parapet and to have it blown off by the blitzkrieg of fundraising applicants; second, and ironically (given one of this book's publishers), because it is now so easy to set up a tax-efficient method of giving using other, less bureaucratic and rigid, means.
- It is inevitable but unfair that the larger metropolitan charities have better access to trusts than their smaller regional counterparts. Many trusts and especially the larger ones are administered in London – so fundraisers there find it easier to make those vital personal connections with their trust donors. If only more trusts were as careful as the Lottery Boards in ensuring that they make grants in the furthest corners of Britain.

Fundraising from tomorrow's trust

Foundations decide which areas they are interested in and then most commonly set up their own project to act in that area; less commonly, although this is happening more and more, foundations sub-contract a non-profit organisation to carry out a defined project. This ties in with the trend in the UK toward a more contractual relationship with grant makers – and is probably where the future of a large part of trust fundraising lies.

If the rich, the entrepreneurs, the philanthropic, continue to create grant-making trusts (and anecdotal evidence suggests that fewer and fewer do so each year), then they can look forward to a cleaner, clearer contractual relationship with their fundraising clients.

PART TWO

The critical importance of research

CHAPTER FOUR

Identifying and locating trusts

Kay Holmes-Siedle

Introduction

Locating, identifying and researching trusts is where any good trust fundraiser begins their work. It is accepted that the job will establish the foundation stones on which the trust programme will be built. The time and planning that will be needed are not so successfully anticipated in many cases. This chapter will help trust fundraisers understand the nature, scope, detail and planning needed to undertake and successfully complete the research phase of a fundraising strategy associated with grant-making trusts.

Before beginning the business of identifying and locating relevant trusts, consider two key facts that need to be borne in mind during the research exercise:

- Organisations called a 'trust', 'foundation' or 'charity' are not necessarily grant-making bodies. They could be tax-avoidance vehicles, government foundations (particularly relevant overseas), or non-grant making to external charities (ie they make grants only to projects they themselves have established).
- Not all trusts that make grants to charities are registered as charitable trusts. This will restrict what can be found out about their activities.

Internal sources – the audit

Most charities, where resources allow, should be undertaking an annual internal audit of the trusts, foundations, settlements and other grant-making bodies that support their charity. Some that are better resourced may of course be able to monitor their trust giving on a more active, say monthly, basis after the first initial audit.

The purpose of the audit is to discover four key facts:

- Does the person responsible for trusts know about all the trusts that support the charity?
- How many trusts that currently support the charity are not listed and described in the main reference sources?
- How quickly does the charity classify a supporter as lapsed? Could this have led to some trusts being prematurely deleted from the charity's trust lists?
- Which trusts in the main reference sources that might be expected to support the charity are apparently not doing so?

AUDIT CASE STUDY

A national charity, which had arranged to have an audit of its trust programme, discovered that trusts were held on several databases, not just on the trust database. In particular, the direct-marketing database held records of many individual trusts, and the corporate database held details of family-run company trusts that would have been more suitably located in the trust programme.

All trusts were then researched to provide information on current objectives and policy, grant budgets, past grants, deadlines and basic trustee information. It was discovered that over 30 per cent of the trusts were not located in the main reference sources and 20 per cent of these were not registered at the Charity Commission. (Three or four of the latter were later revealed to be potentially major givers to the charity.)

Some of the trusts held on the direct-marketing database were categorised as lapsed after two years. Many of the smaller and older trust records could not be recovered. A number of the more generous trusts were found to have been listed in past annual reports.

On examining this trust research, even by eye the charity was able to name trusts that it would have expected or liked to have seen as donors. The charity, therefore, knew that it needed to plan for a phase of serious prospect research (ie to look at new prospective trusts that had not been approached before).

After completing the first part of an audit the trust fundraiser is likely to be faced with a number of dilemmas:

- Where can more information about many of the trusts be found?
- Even allowing for a few trust prospects that immediately come to mind, how can we be sure that we have located all, or most, of the best trusts for the charity?
- I am a resource of one. How can I deal with the massive potential opportunity that exists for my charity?
- Our charity works in such a specialist area; how can I find more trusts?

Establishing a trust research/approach strategy

To answer these questions, it is necessary to establish a clear research strategy. One such is given below, presenting a simplified version of the steps and considerations to be undertaken in recognition of the fact that every charity is different. It should also be remembered that this is a personal view based, however, on successful partnerships with many charities adopting high-value approaches to trusts.

Research strategy for trust fundraising

STAGE 1

- An internal Case for Support document must be analysed and updated, together with brief project and programme summaries.
- Make sure the results of the internal trust audit have been analysed and understood.
- From this intelligence, draw up a trust profile form, including a section for names and in-depth biographies (including interests and soft information) of trustees and other key players.
- Research the top 50 most-generous trusts (by size of existing gift).
- Research a further 50 'best' existing trust donors (for 'best', read 'likely to be of high value with a good match and clear routes to and through them' – specific selection criteria will vary from charity to charity).
- Draw up a first prospect list from X number of external sources, de-duplicating against the trust donor list as you proceed.
- Aim to find and locate a further 50 major trusts (capable of giving £10,000 or above in a single gift).
- Share this top 150 trusts list with key staff and trustees, asking for comments and links.

STAGE 2

Segment the trusts into a gift-value action matrix (a simplified version is given below) by considering a number of factors including:

- Past gifts.
- Top potential of future gifts, based on what the trust had done with your charity and for others.
- The background of the trustees, and the Director/Administrator responsible for each trust.
- The likely level of match between the trust's interests and the charity's Case for Support.

- The religious inclinations of the trustees.
- The existence or warmth of connection between the trust's trustees/director/administrator and the charity's staff or trustees
- The type of trust – personal, family, company, livery, institutional or other.

STAGE 3

Prepare the gift-value matrix along the following lines:

Action matrix

Possible gift value	Action 1–3 months	Action 3–6 months	Action 6–12 months
A £0–£50,000	4	6	10
B £25,001–£50,000	6	10	12
C £10,001–£25,000	2	20	30
D £5,001–£10,000	50	*150	*150
E £1–£5,000	*50	150	*150

* Trusts not yet researched.

Agree individual action plans for A/B/C trustees and trusts in Action 1–3 months. It is particularly crucial to understand the real interests of the trust's trustees. For example, in one case, because of the trustees' interests and known 'modus operandi', picked up in conversation and from press cuttings, a welfare-based Case for Support might be presented, concentrating on the economic arguments for supporting the work. In the case of another trust, it might be clear that what is needed is a much softer, more emotional approach, supported by a meeting with welfare staff and examples of how the project would assist particular families.

Conclusion

The actions required for this phase of research activity are as follows:

- Undertake an internal audit.
- Determine and select the appropriate external sources.
- Undertake research into the top donor prospects and select further cold prospects.
- Understand who makes the key decisions within the trust, and what their backgrounds, likely interests and motivations may be (specialist advice may be needed here).

- Segment the researched trusts constantly against relevant selection criteria.
- Assemble the trust action plan.
- Put into action the 1–3 months individual strategies.

The strategy outlined in this chapter has been tried and tested – individuals are the key to major-gift successes in trust fundraising, and all trust fundraisers should spend time getting to understand what the real concerns and interests of trustees are so as to be able to unlock the true opportunities.

CHAPTER **FIVE**

Preparing projects for trust approaches

Redmond Mullin

Introduction

Trust or foundation approaches, like the rest of fundraising, demand persuasive communications. Therefore their design, together with the selection of projects and of propositions to be made, must start with an understanding of the sources and of the ways in which relations with them can be made optimally productive. The principles stated here apply to not-for-profit organisations of all types and sizes.

Personal contacts

Decisions on trust or foundation grants are made by people, individually or in committee. The majority of trusts (in this chapter, the term 'trusts' includes 'foundations') are channels through which rich individuals and families support not-for-profit causes. But even where the people to be dealt with are trust administrators, or one or more trustees, there is a strong personal element in their decision making. Here are three examples:

- A medium-sized family trust meets twice yearly in its chairman's home in the Cotswolds. Regular grants are reported on and re-appraised; the recipients have been visited by the part-time director; new candidates are proposed for support; all but the smallest have been visited. There is a report by the director on the small grants made at his discretion. If an application is beyond the available means of this trust, other family members who have trusts of their own may decide to collaborate by making grants up to the level needed.
- One of the great English philanthropic families, with several major trusts, meets to consider a major funding application. Father, mother, son and

cousin are there, with the trust's formal administrators; the applicant charity's representatives are there, and the discussion is open. The father argues strongly for the addition of a new element to the programmes proposed. When he questions another aspect of the appeal, his son promptly agrees to fund this from his own trust, to avoid argument. The full, composite grant is made.

- The president of his eponymous foundation, in relation to which he is not even named as a trustee, personally makes the main decisions about grants. Apart from his own projects, this has brought £500,000 in response to a press photograph of a heritage emergency, and payments of development fees, where these could be constructive for the chosen organisations.

The situation with more institutionally managed trusts or foundations is different, but the personal element remains important. This is evident to anyone who has close, perhaps regular, contact with helpful trustees or trust directors. The abstract case is made more vivid, spoken representation of the case more persuasive, when an administrator or trustee has made a visit to see the service or enterprise, or has at least discussed these with key representatives of the charity.

Typologies of trust

One conclusion of a flawed investigation undertaken some years ago (Booth and Mullin, 1976) was that there were significant differences in behaviour between the largest trusts (which had secretariats and included the main 'institutional' trusts), medium-sized trusts (which might or might not be professionally managed) and small trusts (which might be managed by a solicitor or accountant). Those distinctions remain partly valid but do not allow for the impact on any trust's decision-making of actively concerned trustees. Nor do they allow for special factors, such as a founding family's interest in a particular place or region. During the campaign to establish a new university in Lincoln, a virtually unknown, small family trust came forward at a press launch and expressed interest. They had decided to wind up their trust and donated £250,000 to the appeal.

This suggests that any typology of trusts must also take account of some more functionally useful distinctions: between trusts that are more personal or more institutional in character, and those whose decisions are usually or on occasion more personally or bureaucratically determined. A further, critical distinction, given the emphasis placed on personal relations, is between trusts where contact can be established and those where it is unattainable or can even disqualify the applicant from consideration.

Almost regardless of the type of trust concerned, the grant proposition must allow for any strong personal factors there may be that influence grant decisions. Trustees and trust directors, however perfect the criteria and procedures established to guide them, are affected by personal contact and knowledge; and by general prejudices for and against certain causes. Some trust decision makers are prepared to provide funding for difficult objects, such as overheads, salaries and fees; many, initially at least, are not. Most decision makers and influencers will be inclined in favour of great ideas and the programmes that embody them, whether these are on a massive or limited scale.

Aims and targets for trust propositions

As a not-for-profit organisation starts on an appeal or on preparing a set of funding propositions (directed perhaps only to trusts or foundations but more often to individual and corporate sources as well), a not-for-profit organisation must be clear about:

- the outcomes to be achieved through the sums it seeks;
- the overall sum needed to achieve these outcomes;
- the units of support it needs within that overall sum, source by source.

Most frequently, the intended outcomes will be specific: the funding of a building, of equipment, of a project or of a component within a broad programme. Occasionally, the cause itself and the related appeal, strongly declared, may attract significant units of support, which are designated to no specific purpose. However, even if your organisation is one which, with little effort, sometimes attracts large, undesignated support, you must still have articulated a cause of significance, with projects and programmes that will have positive impact on it and which justify the overall appeal target, where there is one. In all instances, the funding proposition must carry the assent of the organisation's key staff and trustees.

Selection of trust sources

The organisation must also decide on the sources of funding it should approach. These may include individuals, often through their trusts, and companies, sometimes through theirs, as well as trusts without such associations. A very simple principle for selection applies here: if the objects stated for a trust or foundation preclude any form of support for this cause or organisation (if the objects are specific concerning the objects to be supported, or restrictive in some way, for example in terms of the people or region that may benefit) then it should not waste their and its time making a grant application.

Normally, the same restriction will apply if the trust's mutable policies preclude an approach – unless the strength of the case or personal contact might change or by-pass those policies.

The funding proposition

It is when the proposition is brought together with the prospective source that the fundraiser's judgement and skill are proved. The proposition should be supported by a business plan and budget projections and will derive from a broad plan of action. It will be articulated for a particular source, or group of sources, and will be specific for them, but should never assume knowledge of the cause or service or use the jargon of medical or social work, or any other specialism. A trust's decision making is likely to involve a process, and applicants for funds are at an advantage if their contact with the source starts positively. Even with those trusts that sometimes give impulsively, the message must be clear and motivating if it is to trigger the response desired.

Allowance must also be made for prejudice as well as ignorance. Certain causes or fields of activity may be instinctively disliked or misunderstood: for example, even in recent years projects for abusers, addicts and homeless single parents have been relatively difficult to fund. The significance of other causes may have been inadequately appreciated: for example, mental disability, epilepsy and AIDS programmes. Then there are the perennially difficult issues relating to overheads, administrative and promotional costs.

Overheads: an issue

Many trusts are more realistic about overheads now than they used to be; and some, such as the main medical research charities and many trusts with primarily academic objects, have agreed common policies on them. Where the argument must be re-entered, some points can be clearly stated. Many organisations have made difficulties for themselves by saying, 'Here are the essential costs of services' and 'There are the administrative and promotional costs' – thus creating a situation where the source may choose to give support to the former but not to the latter. If an organisation has overheads that do not relate directly to services and make these possible, those overheads may legitimately be questioned – whether the services relate to social work, opera, an academic department, a hospital. It can be shown that service can be delivered only if the essential overheads are provided.

Of course, with some more sympathetic and better informed trusts this is not an issue. Quite recently one trust elected specifically to fund a department's overheads because it might be difficult to attract support for them; another trust opted to pay for an organisation's promotional costs; another volunteered to pay for a college's consultancy fees, for a funding study.

None of those negative factors needs be overwhelming, and, with intelligent drafting, an obscure case can be made clear and propositions framed that address ignorance or low awareness. Indeed, the relative unpopularity of a cause or activity can become a positive point in the argument for its support. It may be shown that a valuable project can succeed only if it receives support from this and a few other singularly sympathetic trusts.

As the more mechanical aspects of putting together grant applications to trusts are considered, those related points must be kept in mind. The intention is to deliver a persuasive argument, not to complete a tedious routine. Some trusts or foundations have set forms to be completed for applications – even these give scope for the kind of persuasion, based on the fundraiser's insight, discussed above. However, what should an application contain where a standard application form is not provided?

A variety of forms of approach may be appropriate, all of which involve some measure of creativity. It can also be an advantage (although applications may succeed without it) if there is an established relationship with the trust approached; in such circumstances, there may be discussion about a proposition before any formal approach is made, perhaps with help in formulating the proposition. Yet, even where there is a close relationship, formalities will usually need to be observed in the concluding stages of the application.

The importance of the summary proposition

A crucial component in the application, and the first to be considered by the trustee or administrator to whom the application is sent, is the letter of summary proposition that introduces the application for support. This letter may partly win your argument, or it may lose it. While it does not need to include all the evidence backing your case, it does need to make the case convincingly, allowing for the recipient's likely understanding and attitudes. The letter of summary also needs to be succinct, normally no more than two pages, four at the outside and only if the case were tightly argued. This is not because recipients are lazy; but they are exposed to many applications and need to make their preliminary decisions promptly.

Moreover, if the trust has even simple bureaucratic procedures, the administrator will have to include the summary, but not usually the full documentation, in papers for the trustees' meeting at which a decision may be made. Frequently, the first intention of the application would be to secure an interview or visit from principal decision makers or their representatives. The letter summarising the proposition or accompanying the summary should be signed by someone of standing within the organisation (chairman, director, faculty head, senior curator), not by a fundraiser or someone in the development office, unless that is where the relationship with a trust is well established.

The application needs to be specific on the funding requirement. It is silly to expect a trust to guess the scale and timing of the funding needed from them, and it is a nuisance for the administrator to get back in touch to find out. This means that the sum sought must be stated and justified and also that the incidence of the need be known – for example, in a project spread over three or four years, progressive payments might be appropriate, or a grant two years hence (perhaps for a trust that is currently totally committed) would be as effective as a grant now. It follows that the application must also indicate what funding is anticipated from other sources, to put this grant in context; unless the request is for full funding of a project, salary or capital scheme. Finally, the application must show, in relation to a capital grant, that the enterprise will be viable once established; or, with a revenue project, that after the period of a grant (three or four years, for example) it will have the means to continue.

The letter of summary must cover the main points, even if it is unlikely to be able to cover all the points made above. Because of this, there must usually be a set of supporting papers and documents, to substantiate claims and to provide the detailed information required:

- There will in many cases need to be a full, technical description of the project or programme. Where the application is of some complexity, the trust decision maker may use expert assessors. For a capital programme, architectural plans or equipment specifications will be needed. There may also need to be illustrations, videos or visualisations of buildings or objects to help those decision makers understand what is intended. These support documents may be in the form of a detailed research proposal or of a business prospectus, which is generally preferable to a fine brochure.
- There will usually need to be a statement of vision and mission, a related business plan and projections of anticipated income over three to four years, with its sources; and of expenditure, with its incidence and purposes. This part of the application will include a description of the organisation's aims and achievements.
- Accounts and, if possible, the annual report should be provided. You may need to state and explain the fundraising ratios. Unless these are included, there should be lists of trustees and senior staff, with an outline of the organisation's governance.

Of course, a request for emergency funds cannot observe all these formalities; the passion and weight of argument must succeed in such a case and the sources approached must be selected with imagination and care.

Selection of trusts

For the fundraiser, there must be appropriate selection of trusts, followed by the best possible understanding of prospective trust sources, and of their principal decision makers. Basic research can help with this, using the standard directories and professional agencies, but the information these can provide is limited, particularly where the personal interests and prejudices of these decision makers are concerned. Organisations that already have good relations with at least a few trusts start with an advantage; those that do not may be able to get advice on the attitudes and behaviour of trusts and foundations which they believe might respond to them. If such information is not available, an organisation has to make quite raw decisions on who might respond to a capital appeal for: buildings or equipment; research or medical or welfare projects; a university department or arts body.

External factors

Government policies periodically change the availability of statutory funding for crucial categories of people in need: the homeless, lone parents, people needing expensive treatments for cancer and other conditions, young people needing funds for secondary or tertiary education excluded from public support, for whatever reason. Many trustees have felt that they should not respond to pressures created by the removal of support which, it is perceived, government should provide. They are then confronted with people in desperate situations who will not receive the support they need unless these trustees, perhaps exceptionally concerned and enlightened, change their minds and decide to provide it.

Lottery funds are making often impossible demands on organisations without fundraising achievement or skills to raise sometimes millions of pounds in partnership funds. One thoughtful trust, having started by saying its grants would be conditional on a Lottery offer, has latterly decided it will provide no partnership funding, because the volume of demand is too great.

Conclusion

Good fundraising changes the realities. Some individual organisations may be able to change the policies of a few trusts; otherwise there needs to be wider-scale persuasion, involving many organisations in a common cause. The trusts have their own, formal and informal channels for communication and discussion. It is possible for charities collectively to make representations to the more thoughtful trusts.

The key principle here, as with all sources for fundraising, is that decisions are made not by process but by people.

Should we have a trust department? – an issue

There are structural matters to be considered by any organisation that undertakes trust fundraising. Most trusts are the vehicles used by individuals or families for their philanthropic transactions, so that there needs to be good understanding of who makes a trust's decisions before approaches are made. The same is true of some corporate trusts. So should an organisation have a trust fundraising department? Perhaps alongside major donor and corporate departments?

There can be some serious consequent problems if it does, unless it defines roles and relationships very clearly. The question is where productive relations can most effectively be established: within a major private or corporate support function or a specific trust function? Does the trust fundraising department operate as an information-providing, co-ordinating function with direct responsibility for trusts that would not otherwise be covered, and perhaps for Lottery applications?

In some organisations there may be many possible starting points for trust approaches. It is generally counter-productive to create a situation in which major trusts may receive many simultaneous approaches from the same organisation. This does not mean that all approaches should be from head office – in many instances an approach from some other point may be more effective; but the approaches do need to be co-ordinated. Is a department necessary for this?

CHAPTER SIX

Planning approaches

Graham Collings

Introduction

A fundraiser once maintained he had a 'magic letter' for grant-giving trusts. The approach was so good that it brought results every time: everybody should use it, or something similar, because it was a sure-fire winner with any trust. His magic approach was a very short, very emotive letter about a very emotive project. It did bring in quite a lot of donations, but they were small, and he had conveniently forgotten about all the non-responders and polite refusals. It certainly wouldn't have worked with a different charity.

The truth is that there is no one 'right' approach. Trusts are all different, and the right approach is the one that is appropriate for that particular recipient. The administrator of a large, highly professional trust in its own offices has a very different viewpoint from the trustee of the small family trust who opens your letter at the breakfast table. How then to organise approaches on a worthwhile scale without having to manage hundreds of different versions?

The answer is that trusts don't expect every approach to be an individually crafted jewel: they expect it to be personalised, but they know that any sensible grant seeker will be applying to many other trusts as well.

Segmenting trusts for approaches

The most practical way of managing approaches is to segment the trusts you want to approach into a number of groups. Each group of trusts can then get a similar type of approach. For example, a national charity with on-going needs might segment its trust constituency as follows:

- smaller previous supporters, giving a few hundred pounds or less as a general donation per year;

- larger previous supporters, giving in four or five figures;
- prospective supporters, new prospects, who could also be segmented by size;
- project supporters, who prefer to fund only specific types of project or aspects of the work;
- special contacts, where there is a contact or special relationship with a trustee or administrator.

For a major capital appeal in, say, Manchester, starting from scratch, the categories might be:

- major potential supporters around Manchester;
- major potential supporters further afield;
- trusts where there is a contact with appeal-committee members or project staff;
- those known to fund capital projects of a similar type;
- those where a trustee is known to have an interest in this type of cause.

There could be other categories: if you have a team of people working on trust fundraising, you may have the time to segment and personalise further. If you are doing trust fundraising on your own, you may not, and it's important to keep things manageable.

Having segmented relevant trusts into groups, you need to think about which is the right project or 'package' to send to each group. If you're starting trust fundraising from scratch, the best way is to set out your projects and possible funding packages first, and then see how they match up with trusts' interests, bearing in mind all the different aspects of your charity's work (some trusts, for example, will be quite happy to fund the telephone bill or the cost of a consultancy).

If you are already raising funds from trusts, it is easier to pick out projects and packages fitting the interests of trusts you already know. Their donations, and in some cases their rejection letters, will give you an idea of what they like to fund.

Avoid the temptation of distorting the nature of your charity's work to make it fit the objects of trusts. Many charities, for example, try to present work in the social welfare or health field as educational in order to attract funds from trusts with education in their remit, but these trusts usually have a very clear idea of what they mean by education, and trustees are frequently adept at picking out and rejecting such applications.

The timing of your approach

Most trusts meet infrequently, so trust deadlines should be a key factor in your planning. Are there any relevant trusts with a once-a-year meeting coming up soon? Are there some whose meeting dates are too late or too soon for your project needs? The lead time between application and result is commonly 3–6 months, so if your project needs to be fully funded before that, you should not depend on trust funding. Some large trusts now operate a waiting list so that, even if you are applying in time for their March meeting, they may not be able to consider you until June.

Approaching trusts should be a year-round process, not the subject of occasional forays. You will need a schedule setting out the deadlines for relevant trusts month by month, matching these up with your project deadlines. Build into the schedule the times when you need to send updates, re-approach, suggest visits, or claim future instalments of a grant.

Planning the programme – the trust fundraising cycle

DEVELOPING THE CASE

- Use your charity's case statement and other literature to identify key facts and arguments that may be used in approaching trusts.
- Identify what you need funds for and where trust funding – as distinct from funding from other sources – fits.
- Formulate projects suitable for trust funding.
- Draft materials for approaches that are relevant for trusts (don't forget your accounts).

RESEARCHING THE SOURCES

- Research trusts that look appropriate in terms of objects, areas of benefit, deadlines, etc.
- Research your other supporters and any links with trusts.
- Send for application forms or guidelines where available.
- Identify any contacts among your charity's own trustees, patrons or committee members.
- Give a priority to your hit-list of trusts in terms of deadlines, best prospects, good contacts.

PREPARING AND MAKING THE APPROACHES

- Plan a manageable programme of approaches.
- Make phone calls to elicit further information where possible.

- Arrange for your charity's patrons/trustees to talk to selected trustees/administrators.
- Arrange any events to attract trustees and administrators.
- Write the application, taking into account all the information gained about the trust.
- Monitor the programme of approaches; check deadlines.

REVIEWING AND FOLLOWING UP

- Record all responses.
- Evaluate response rates from different types of trust or different types of approach.
- Follow up or provide updates where needed.
- Say thank you.
- Update the programme of future contacts, updates, approaches.

Most trusts expect you to apply no more frequently than once a year, so you can plan on approaching and re-approaching them with a three-year rolling programme according to their responses. A rejection or no reply the first time round does not necessarily mean you have wasted your time. Your approach may simply have come at a time when the trust was under financial pressure, or had too many applications in a similar field to yours.

Unless the rejection is firm and clear, it's worth following a 'three strikes and out', policy of approaches before giving up on any trust prospect. A three-year programme of approaches for a group of trusts would probably run as follows:

Year 1 response	Year 2 action	Year 3 action
No reply	Re-approach	Re-approach
Firm no, not eligible	No action	No action
Standard rejection	Re-approach	Re-approach
Yes	Update, re-approach	Re-approach

In all cases, watch out for changes in trusts' policies in subsequent years, or for new projects run by your charity that might give you a better chance.

After three years of rejections or no response from a trust it's probably wise to call it a day. Even so, continue to monitor its operations, as situations can and do change.

The exploratory phone call

Much of the detail on deadlines, as well as that on objects and guidelines, can be gleaned from desk research, using directories and your records of past trust supporters. One important source not to be overlooked, however, is the exploratory phone call. There is much information to be gained by this method, as well as the chance to sell your cause a little, or establish a rapport. Some examples of what you may be able to find out, beyond what's already given in a directory entry, are shown below.

Ten things to find out in an exploratory phone call

1 Date of next trustees meeting and deadline for applications
2 Up-to-date address or contact name
3 Any recent changes to policy or priorities
4 Awareness of your organisation
5 Usual level and type of donation
6 Frequency of donations
7 Whether capital costs, salaries, etc are supported
8 Amount/type of information needed in the application
9 Which of your projects is most relevant
10 How to handle any contacts with trustees

Some trusts give a phone number; others don't. Where a firm of solicitors or accountants are listed for correspondence it's usually quite easy to find their number. Of course if they state, as a few do, 'No phone calls', you will probably create annoyance by phoning.

Normally you will be speaking to an administrator, not a trustee. With many of the trusts on your hit list this may be the only point of contact, and it's worth preparing such calls carefully. Having a checklist of points and a proforma for each call is a useful idea.

A USEFUL PHONE CALL

A livery company had supported an environmental charity for some years with annual donations of £300. Just before the normal time of applying, the fundraiser rang the administrator to check the details and see if there were any changes. The administrator said that there had been a major change of policy, and the company would henceforth be supporting a much smaller number of charities working with disabled or unemployed people. The charity had several projects with unemployed people, and what would have been a general application (with a much reduced chance of success) was changed to focus on this work. The result was a donation of £5,000.

Using contacts – does it work?

You should by now have some basic information on the trusts you want to approach. You've done the homework on the projects that are relevant. The next step is to find out how best to make the approaches and, particularly, what contacts the charity has that could be used in the process.

Personal contacts or special relationships with trustees can make a huge difference to success. As in other forms of fundraising, the personal approach from someone in the same peer group is a good way of influencing the outcome of your application. But it needs to be organised carefully and with tact. Let's consider how and why it works with trusts.

Nowadays it is no longer simply a question of an appeals committee chairman nobbling an old school friend at the golf club. Trusts are more sophisticated than that, and carefully thought-out giving policies are no longer circumvented by use of the old school tie or a free meal. However, trustees are still capable of being influenced by judicious approaches or endorsements from people they know and respect. This happens quite commonly with those trusts that are primarily the vehicle for giving money from one individual or family and that have a wide remit; it is less frequent with those trusts, large or small, that have established clear policies and procedures for grant making. Trustees still listen to people they know and respect, perhaps to whom they owe a favour, but the application still has to be relevant and well put together.

The big pitfall in talking to trustees before making your application is the danger of upsetting the administrator. Trust administrators in many of the larger trusts now wield considerable power and may object to unfair 'string pulling', or approaches made behind their back. If you are planning to use a contact with a trustee, make sure that it won't be counter-productive with the trust concerned. The best policy is to be open with the administrator about any special link you have, and respect their advice on how to handle it. Most turn out to be quite relaxed about a charity making contact with a trustee they know, and pleased to have been informed that it is happening.

What is also happening nowadays is that many trusts, faced with an ever-increasing flood of applications, are paying more attention to those that involve people they know. This is not a reference to celebrity patrons nor solely to the great and good, but to committee members, trustees or key staff known to have a good track record in the charity or with a similar project elsewhere.

A phrase appearing ever more often in directory entries is 'trustees prefer to support those charities where they have special knowledge or association'. The meaning is usually 'we cannot possibly make accurate judgements between so many equally deserving causes, so we prefer to back those where someone we know and respect is involved.'

Planning for the best approach

From the fundraiser's point of view, what all this means is that it is worth while adding an extra element to the application process, to identify and make use of the contacts you have. The steps in doing this are as follows:

- Produce lists of your main trust targets with the names of trustees and administrators.
- Distribute them to committee members, key staff, patrons, long-standing supporters (ie those likely to move in the right circles).
- Ask these people, either individually or as a group, to identify those they know.
- Collate and explore these contacts further to find those that are worth using.
- Organise approaches using these contacts.

This may seem a laborious process, and you may well meet with initial apathy. Few people think they will know any trustees, but few trustees mention this aspect of their lives in casual conversation and this exercise frequently yields surprisingly good results. It works well in local campaigns, where the networks are likely to be strong; it also works well if you can take the trouble to research a list relevant to the audience – for example, showing a list of trusts with a medical remit or with medically qualified trustees to a group of health professionals.

Be careful to keep people interested and motivated. When these steps have been carried out as a dull administrative task in a big appeal, the results have been poor: one example that failed to enthuse people involved sending out a huge list of names in the post and ordering recipients to mark up and return the list within two weeks (or else!). This is one of those areas of fundraising where you have to keep things simple and light hearted, and above all to remind everyone of the cause and why this part of the process is so important. Try making it more interesting by bringing people together as a group, providing refreshments, and creating a worthwhile session of brainstorming and reminiscence.

It is always worth while planning some initiatives to identify and make use of a trust contact, or just to tempt a trustee or administrator out of their lair. There is a natural reluctance to agree to meetings with fundraisers, or to pay a visit to a potential grant seeker, but, if the opportunity is relevant and interesting, the response is often quite good. How do you create such opportunities? Here are some examples:

- A community centre in Bristol organised an Open Day with exhibitions and displays of its work.
- Through the efforts of a committee member who was a retired oil company executive, a small disability charity was given the use of a plush suite in the company's prestigious London headquarters to hold an evening reception.
- A medical charity organised a lecture by an eminent scientist on some important new research.
- The royal patron of a conservation charity was persuaded to host a select launch party for a new appeal.
- The new director of a national charity arranged a private lunch to introduce himself and gather feedback from funders about the charity.
- A charity for homeless people organised a simple opening ceremony at a new night shelter to say thank you to the trusts who had supported it.

Trustees and trust administrators responded well to all these occasions because they were convenient, because the subject matter was of broad relevance, or simply because their interest was aroused. The opening of a night shelter might not seem an attractive event, but the trustees attending were solicitors and other professional people who were absolutely fascinated to get a glimpse of a world so different from their own.

Face-to-face contact in these situations does not guarantee success, but it can make a lot of difference: motivation is built up and the often very limited understanding a trustee has of your charity's work can be extended dramatically. From the trustee's point of view, they get a much fuller picture of the charity than a letter or application form could ever provide, and they may be able to meet key people involved. Socially, it may offer the opportunity to meet people from a totally different sector of society.

The fundraiser's job on all such occasions is to be the planner and the choreographer, making sure that the event is as relevant and attractive as possible for trusts, inviting the most appropriate guests, seeing that all the important introductions are made and that key messages are conveyed and relationships developed. Afterwards the task is to pick up on and follow up every snippet of information or feedback gained from the guests. The most casual aside from a trustee could be vital information for the formal approach: one suggestion that you should apply for £10,000 rather than £1,000 would easily make the whole thing worth while.

Good records are vital in trust fundraising. Outcomes from any occasion such as the above need to be recorded carefully with other information about the trust, not in some soon-forgotten file marked 'Chairman's Reception'. The responses to your day-to-day phone calls, the feedback from conversations between your director or committee member and any trustee, all need to be recorded alongside the other research information you have gleaned. Always refer back to the records of the individual trust when it comes to the formal approach. There could be some small but essential point to remember, such as the format of the application, or a major issue such as the timing or amount to ask for. Even in such a volatile world as that of trusts, if you plan and prepare your approaches properly, the chances of success will be greatly improved.

PART THREE

Approaching grant-making trusts

CHAPTER SEVEN

Making first contact

Tim Finn

Introduction

The project is now defined, the trust research complete, the approach strategy planned with care. From this point onwards the human factor in trust fundraising will become paramount in ensuring a successful outcome to the campaign.

It is helpful, at this stage, to remember just why the human factor in approaches to trusts plays such an important part in the results.

It might be supposed that, equipped with all the documentary support compiled during the preparatory work, you are already in a position to despatch excellent written applications for your researched trusts to consider. In all logic, these should result in the arrival of plentiful grants.

Not so. A purely written technique, a correspondence campaign, will always produce a far smaller return than a campaign that takes full account of the many personal elements at work in trusts' grant decisions.

In order to understand why this is the case, it will be helpful to see the subject of grant applications, not from the fundraiser's perspective, but through the eyes of one of the trusts targeted. A moment's reflection will then show just how human – how non-documentary – many of the factors at work are.

> ### CASE STUDY OF AN IMAGINARY GRANT-MAKING TRUST
>
> Let us take as an illustration the case of an imaginary trust of medium to large size, the Knatchpole Trust, whose giving objects cover a range of general, charitable themes.
>
> The Knatchpole Trust has £1 million to distribute in grants each year. Since it seeks to donate money rather than spend its funds unnecessarily, its staff is

limited to just two people: these are the correspondent, Mr Protheroe, and his secretary. The Knatchpole Trust receives 25 times more applications than it can possibly support. As many as 70 separate grant submissions arrive in an average week.

Mr Protheroe is a conscientious man. He endeavours to assess all the cold, written applications in the light of his trust's objectives. In truth, however, this is a near impossible task. This very morning his mailbox has yielded no fewer than 15 requests, with subject matters as diverse as Cambwick Castle Restoration, Student Homeless Outreach, the Botswana Herons' Egg Society, and a children's playgroup in Polperro. All of these theoretically qualify for consideration; as to the merits of any one versus any other, it will be very difficult to make a judgement between them.

Suddenly the phone rings. It is the trust's chairman, Sir Hector Knatchpole.

'Look here, I've just heard about a wonderful cause and I think we ought to support it. I've told them to write in. There should be something on your desk this morning.'

'It wouldn't be Student Homeless Outreach, or Cambwick Castle Restoration, perhaps?' Mr Protheroe enquires.

'No. No. Nothing like that. It's herons' eggs in Botswana. Put it on the short-list, will you? I think we need to look at this one pretty seriously. Far too little is being done about the Botswana heron, in my opinion.'

Sir Hector has clearly received a personal approach.

This example illustrates a broad, general principle: where applications are of apparently equal merit, trustees will often rely on the recommendations of dependable acquaintances for guidance on which charitable causes they should support.

This is why the human factor is so important. In order to make personal approaches to trusts, you will sometimes need to enlist specialist 'helpers' – sometimes called patrons – to open doors for you.

Final documentary preparation

Before assuming that your documentary preparations are complete, you would be wise to make sure that your researched material is not just compre-hensive, but that it is also presented in an accessible format. Indigestible trust information can be very daunting if it has not been carefully tailored to meet its human audience.

For the purpose of discussions with helpers, prepare four separate lists of researched trusts, each strictly limited to 50 trusts at most. An interested helper will gladly consider 50 trusts and may then go on to consider 50 more – but it is important to feed the information through to the helper in manageable tranches.

The four lists of trust will normally be:

- major trusts – of national importance;
- City livery companies – closely resembling major trusts;
- local and regional trusts – within your catchment area;
- specialist trusts – within your field of charitable work.

This restricted information should then be typed on to A4 sheets in landscape format and presented under five columns, as follows:

- Column 1 – trust name, address, and correspondent;
- Column 2 – annual grant income;
- Column 3 – trustees in full, listed by name;
- Column 4 – objectives, briefly noted in up to ten words;
- Column 5 – other special features, very briefly noted.

Now you are ready to meet your first helper and ask for assistance with personal introductions.

What type of helper do you need?

Major trusts

The type of person you will need to help you with introductions to major trusts is far from obvious to those who have not conducted a trust grants campaign before.

You would initially expect that a leading businessman or an eminent technical specialist would be just the sort of supporter to secure the attention of a trust. The reality, however, is that it is friendship and not career success that is the key to good introductions. Professional eminence is altogether a secondary factor.

So how do you identify helpers with such an unspecific profile as this – the possible friends of listed, unknown trustees? The answer is that a good many of the trustees on your list will be far from the unknowns you suppose them to be.

Glance for a moment at your list of 50 major trusts. Whatever method you have used to compile this list, you will at once recognise that a significant proportion of the names qualify for the unofficial title 'The great and the good'.

Here is a cross-section of that well-disposed and socially eminent group of persons whose lives are quietly spent in discreet service to their country and community. Nowhere are these old-fashioned virtues better represented than on the boards of the leading grant-making trusts.

It now becomes clear what type of helpers you will need – they should be people who move in these distinguished circles. If you can find several helpers of this type then, between them, they will be able to identify contacts at a great many of the major trusts you have listed.

Local and specialist trusts

Local and specialist trusts are less likely to have distinguished persons on their boards, although there are many exceptions to this general rule.

Evidently, in order to make introductions on the basis of friendship in these cases, further helpers will need to be found, whose lives interact with the trustees concerned – helpers who are socially active within a particular county or neighbourhood and who will assist you with local trusts. Where the trust specialises in your particular field of work, then you will need to recruit external helpers who are familiar with this area of charitable activity.

How do you recruit your helpers?

Major trusts

Faced with the unfamiliar task of recruiting distinguished helpers for your charitable approaches, your first reaction may be to hold your head in your hands. The chances of succeeding in this objective seem slender, even non-existent.

The problem is more imaginary than real, and the first point to note is that your task will have been made much easier if you have already laid the groundwork for this recruitment before the recruitment drive itself is mounted. In a perfect world you will already have invited the Mayor, the Bishop, the Lord Lieutenant or other leaders to become patrons of your charity. Where such steps have been taken, then the business of finding further active, eminent helpers to make your trust approaches is greatly simplified. People will do much to support the causes that their local leaders have espoused.

Let us assume, however, that you are starting your helper recruitment from scratch, and that you have no honorary patrons who could attract them to your cause. We will also assume, for illustrative purposes, that your charity or your project is sited within a defined geographical area. Should that not be the case, then the basic principles of recruitment will need to be adapted to the circumstances, even if they will not fundamentally change.

People active in public life are often confident and fully aware of the role expected of them in making supportive introductions on behalf of a range of good causes. For the volunteer concerned, this often acts as an important element in cementing their own aspirations in relation to personal esteem and social cachet.

Given the fundraiser's ability to support the administrative and research functions associated with volunteer-led introductions, the task facing the volunteer will not be at all daunting.

Indeed, it is hard to imagine any role that is capable of achieving so good an effect from so modest an outlay of valuable time. All that you will ask your helpers to do is to write a small number of introductory letters to acquaintances who happen to be the trustees of major trusts. There are no further duties – no committee meetings, minutes or action points beyond the simple, letter-writing task.

If you do not yet know which eminent persons live within your area, then you have been working up to now in a vacuum of your own choosing. Nevertheless, a good social directory, such as Debrett's *People of Today* will supply the information you need.

Now write a letter.

Your first letter, let us say, is to a local baronet, Sir Jasper Hackforth. You have not met Sir Jasper before, nor does he know of you.

The letter you write to Sir Jasper will of course be courteous and, necessarily, rather long. In it you will summarise your work, stressing that he and you are near neighbours, and touching judiciously on the task that you have in mind for him. Spell out that, in helping you, he will not become entangled in your day-to-day concerns and administration. There will be no burdensome involvement other than the opening of one or two doors in the direction of grant-making trusts.

Sir Jasper may, of course, decline to assist you, but that is not the usual response. It is more likely that he will write back with friendly and genuine modesty:

'I should be happy to see you if you wish, although I am inclined to doubt whether I could be of any use. Nonetheless, if you feel that I may be of some help to you in your charitable work, do please give me a ring to see if we can find a moment to meet.'

So, your first helper has agreed to see you. The meeting you arrange should ideally be at Sir Jasper's house. This will cause as little disruption as possible to his normal day. Such considerations should be a constant feature of all your work with your distinguished helpers.

Local and specialist trusts

In recruiting local and specialist helpers, the same principles apply: the same courtesies, the same care in using your supporters' time sparingly and to good effect.

For approaches to local and regional trusts, you can enlist the help of solicitors, accountants or estate agents who know the neighbourhood well. For approaches to specialist trusts, your own knowledge of the field will normally suggest some well-disposed and widely respected advisers.

The meeting with the helper

There is nothing to be feared in a meeting with an eminent helper, or indeed with any helper. The fact that Sir Jasper has agreed to make time available is already proof of his kindly disposition towards you. Provided you have prepared yourself well and provided that you do not trespass too far on your helper's freely given time, your meeting will be successful.

In harmony with Sir Jasper's natural pace, therefore, you should discreetly move the business forward, aiming for a meeting of no more than 45 minutes:

- First, re-cap on the work of your charity and on the purpose of your visit, so that Sir Jasper is reminded of your objectives.
- Second, hand Sir Jasper your project document for future reading. He may glance at this briefly and ask some simple questions.
- Third, hand Sir Jasper your list of major trusts and draw his attention to the names of the trustees.
- Fourth, as Sir Jasper comments on the list, make brief, rapid notes of his remarks on your own master copy. A digest of this information should be confirmed back to him later.

In most cases you will find that, starting from a standpoint of diffidence, Sir Jasper will soon become charmed to find that he does indeed recognise several of the names listed. He may even become intrigued and enthusiastic: 'Is that the father or the son? If it's the father, I could certainly drop him a line. I don't suppose you could find out, could you?' Take a note of these points: they will be very important for the future.

By the time he has gone through the list of major trusts, Sir Jasper may have found, say, five acquaintances to whom he could write. If his interest remains high, then the list of livery companies may be handed to him, and subsequently the other two lists also. However, it is very important that you judge your helper's stamina wisely. The fun of spotting acquaintances on a list can soon become a chore if you persevere insensitively.

By the time the meeting ends, seven people have been identified whom Sir Jasper knows well. There are also three further possibilities on whom more research work needs to be done.

At this point it is important to relieve Sir Jasper of every possible burden, even though he may be keen to get down to his tasks straightaway. Undertake to draft the letters that he will sign. Send Sir Jasper a note of the meeting, and reassure him that at this stage he need do nothing more than wait to hear from you with a summary of the next steps to be taken.

Follow-up on a meeting with a helper

Detailed and accurate follow-up is necessary after every meeting with a helper. The follow-up also needs to be succinct, identifying all the nuances in as few words as possible. Once a full panel of helpers is at work, the need for precision becomes even more important. Several helpers will know the same trustee, and it is essential that recommendations are not accidentally duplicated.

Immediately on return to your office, therefore, summarise your discussions in a letter to Sir Jasper. Where additional research is required, do this at once and include the results in the summary.

Attached to the summary is the letter of recommendation that you are now asking Sir Jasper to write to his acquaintances. One sample letter will occasionally be sufficient. More frequently, however, several letters will have to be prepared, because there will be special circumstances to refer to in a number of cases.

The golden rules are:

- Sir Jasper must write from his own home, on his own notepaper and, if possible, in his own hand. Everything that indicates personal effort will reinforce his message.
- Sir Jasper should write a short friend-to-friend letter, *not* a formal application. He may change the wording you have suggested just as he pleases, but you will find that he will normally follow your original text fairly closely.
- Sir Jasper must write to his trustee friend at home. Letters sent to business addresses, clubs or the House of Lords are less effective, although sometimes unavoidable.

- The tone and wording of the letter must be distinctly more heartfelt than your natural British reserve would at first suggest: 'For much of my life I have admired the work of this small group', etc.
- The letter, though it is by no means a formal application, must close with a request that a formal application may be sent. 'All I would ask, Hector, is that my friends at this charity might prepare a formal application for the Knatchpole Trust to consider. Nothing would please me more than to have your encouragement for this to be done.'

The outcome of the helper's work

Friend-to-friend letters, although they work very well in the trust fundraising field, cannot, of course, work every time. If the helper has written before on several charitable themes, then the impact will be reduced. If the helper is more of a passing acquaintance than a friend, then that too will be reflected in the reply. Finally, you must always remember that trust funds are under constant and increasing pressure. It may simply not be possible for trustees to make an award in some instances, however much they may wish to do so.

At its best, however, the method described has the singular effect of by-passing the initial assessment stage in a trust's deliberations, thus ensuring a smooth passage of your case from the letter box to the shortlist.

In response to Sir Jasper's recommendation, his friend Sir Hector Knatchpole replies:

Dear Jasper,

Many thanks for your note about the Botswana Herons' Egg Society.

We will certainly see if we can help. Funds are a bit stretched at present, but it does sound a most deserving cause. Do please ask your friends to write to our Correspondent, Marcus Protheroe, with a full application. We next meet in May.

Yours ever,

Hector.

All now depends on the quality of the formal application itself.

CHAPTER EIGHT

Making the application

Anthony Clay

Planning to avoid rejection

The key to avoiding rejection is to have done everything needed before the final moment when you make the formal application. Whenever possible, the application should arrive after several previous communications have been held with the trust and should, ideally, reflect this earlier work. Typically, an accompanying letter should be along the lines of: 'Following our previous conversations and your visit on 13 August 1999, we are now enclosing our formal application to the trustees who, we understand, are meeting on 22 October 1999', possibly with a further paragraph of explanation, for example: 'You will see that the amount we are asking for is the sum needed to ensure that this project happens.'

Sometimes, it will not have been possible to go through all these prepara-tions. The size of the trust's grants may be so small that the time and effort in preliminary work may not be justified. Many trusts simply refuse to engage in any discussions or preliminaries, insisting on a written application only.

Whatever the earlier work you have been able to do, it will be absolutely essential to follow the trust's rules and procedures to the letter.

The trust's requirements

The policies and application rules can be flexible or rigid, but frequently reflect the personalities of the trustees. Here are two examples:

McClaren Foundation

(Objects include animal welfare, war disabled, regimental charities, refugees from communism, distressed widows and pensioners of the pro-fessional income group, general charitable purposes.)

...Enjoyable expeditions overseas for students on the pretext of some scientific investigation of doubtful utility that claims to compress into 2–3 weeks scientific work that will require a period of years, or to assist for a few weeks a native population...to carry out simple construction works that they are far better able to carry out themselves...are not entertained...The Trustees will use their best endeavours not to be prejudiced against an application that uses the jargon evolved by the new Welfare Industry such as 'caring', 'underprivileged' and 'deprived'.

Christie Charitable Trust

(Objects are general charitable purposes. To promote medical research and education.)

Assistance is given to special causes and charitable bodies of special interest to the Trustees. Appeals of the 'expensive glossy brochure' variety are neither welcomed nor considered.

Some trusts will be happy to let you have written instructions about what they require; others simply leave it up to you. Some have very detailed forms to complete; others ask only for a short letter.

Deciding how much to ask for

Deciding how much to ask for is a very difficult point. Clearly, you must not ask for more than what is needed. Beyond that basic fact, however, you should be primarily guided by the results of any research that you have been able to carry out into the trust's income and the money it has available for grant distribution. Sometimes the published directories will give an indication of typical grant sizes that can be helpful.

One rule of thumb is that you should ask for up to 10 per cent of the trust's annual grants figure, but this can be misleading because much will depend upon how many grants are being made and what their average size is. Occasionally, trusts may give away capital, which could result in exceptionally large one-off grants; benefactors may top up a trust to enable special grants to be made; a trust may have received an extraordinary income in the last year; from time to time trusts are wound up altogether, sometimes distributing all the assets to one beneficiary.

It is not a good idea to try to pool projects in order to reach the highest possible grant size that a trust has ever made. There should be much better matching of individual project to trust and vice versa.

The application itself

Although to many people this is the key element in the process, what really matters, as explained above, is what precedes that application.

Nevertheless, there are several important points to remember:

- Always follow the trust's instructions.
- Do not make handwritten applications unless they are beautifully legible.
- Be clear and precise.
- Answer all the key questions such as who will benefit, how the project will be evaluated, what other funding you are getting.
- Make sure that the application is on time: send it by special delivery if necessary.

Finally, it is a good idea to check that the application has actually been received, particularly because this presents an opportunity to make any final points that you feel may sway the arguments in your favour.

The notes below, from a very experienced trust administrator, are most useful.

Notes to applicants, from a trust administrator

(With grateful thanks to Clive Marks of the Lord Ashdown Charitable Trust)

FIVE IDEAS FOR THE WASTE-PAPER BASKET

- The blanket appeal
- Dear Sir/Madam
- Very glossy – shock tactics
- 'Exciting', 'unique', 'desperate', 'exciting new challenge', 'unless you help, he/she will die'
- Undated

SIZE AND APPEARANCE

- 1–2 sides A4, typed
- Come to the point quickly
- An appropriate photograph
- No jargon – good English, no acronyms
- Get someone to 'play devil's advocate' when the application is complete

FIVE IDEAS FOR THE CONTENT

- Say who else is helping you
- What you completed last year – what has to be done now

- The size of your organisation – the size of your staff (paid and volunteers)
- Numbers help
- Newspaper cuttings

THE FIGURE

This is the most difficult part of the letter

- It must come early on.
- Be specific.
- If very large, don't write until a personal contact is made on a trustee-to-trustee basis.
- If you are raising £500,000 for building or equipment, explain how you intend to maintain that asset in future years.

Applications: a trust's view

Des Palmer, formerly of the Allied Dunbar Charitable Trust

What to do; what not to do

Applying to charitable trusts can be something of a lottery. There is no perfect way, there is no formula, no magic phrase that guarantees success; it is an exercise that in some ways is as much a gamble as picking a set of numbers on a football coupon. For the grant seeker, however, there are some general 'dos' and 'don'ts' which, if followed, are more likely to result in success. Far from being the construct of a fundraising theorist, these guidelines are derived from the daily working experience of the author and other long-serving trust officers.

A few words on the grant-giving trust world

The grant-making trust world has some truly outstanding trusts, managed by wise and imaginative trustees and with capable and objective trust administrators who delight in visiting applicants. Alas, the overall picture is more generally of cautious and hard-pressed trustees and part-time or unpaid administrators.

The overwhelming majority of the UK's 8,800 trusts are run by volunteers. This means there are no paid part-time, let alone full-time, staff to open mail, read applications, reject the majority, seek information on a few, travel hundreds of miles to visit, write reports, prepare agendas, organise meetings, write minutes, send rejection letters, send letters announcing success, write and send cheques, monitor and report back on grants, prepare annual reports, fill in innumerable questionnaires, answer the telephone, etc. Even when there are staff, they are invariably hard pressed and face an increasing deluge of applications. The first lesson for the grant seeker, therefore, is 'Treat each trust as a unique organisation'.

The 'dos' of applying

The 'dos' divide themselves into four sections: preliminary work, the general principles of an application, the specific detail required in an application, and what to do afterwards.

Preliminary work

- Think ahead. Work out your organisation's income and expenditure, not just for this year but for next year, and even the year after. All fundraising takes time; if you want to avoid financial crises, plan well ahead. Develop a written fundraising strategy.
- Research the trust world – find out about funding programmes, geographical areas of benefit and the names of correspondents. Do use up-to-date directories (eight years after changing its name, the then Allied Dunbar Charitable Trusts still received letters addressed to the Hambro Life Charitable Trust).
- Find out, by using the directories, your local CVS or Charities Information Bureau (if you have one) or from other grant seekers, how each trust prefers to be approached. Some encourage informal telephone calls, whereas for others this would be the fastest road to rejection. Some prefer an initial written outline, some a detailed application; others insist that you use their application form.

You must be clear about what you want and why you want it, and you must find out as much as you can about the trusts you are planning to approach. Trust in-trays are full of mis-directed applications: this is a waste of trust time, but it is also a waste of yours. There is little point, indeed there is no point at all, in a youth club in the western corner of Wiltshire applying to a trust whose only aim is to 'alleviate poverty among former schoolteachers in Yorkshire'. Look for trusts that can fund only in your area, or that express a preference for doing so. Seek out those interested in your field of work and the individuals (or users) who benefit from it.

The general principles of an application

Make sure that your application is:

- **Concise**. The back windows of many cars advertise the driver's peccadilloes such as 'Windsurfers do it standing up', 'Vicars do it on their knees' and 'Young farmers do it in their wellies'. Trust administrators have engraved on their hearts 'Grant administrators like it done on two sides of A4'.
- **Attractively presented**, but not so flash as to ring alarm bells about profligate spending on fundraising.

- **On time.** 'Sorry I can't make your deadline: the typist is sick/headquarters haven't sent the accounts/the chairman is on holiday, etc.' Trust administrators set deadlines not because they are training for a career in the civil service but because they have a timetable to keep to. It is the trustees who decide which applications to support at meetings that may be held once a year, once a quarter or once a month. A trust administrator needs sufficient time to assemble applications, draw up agendas and circulate papers.
- **Addressed to the right person**, with the name and address correctly spelt. Joel Joffe, the former Chairman of the Allied Dunbar Charitable Trust, has been addressed as Noel, Toffe, Coffee and Joff. Des Palmer simply hate being addressed as Des Wilson. Jerry Marston, now the head of Public Affairs at Littlewoods plc, still reacts very badly to being mistaken on paper for an ageing Merseyside pop singer.
- **Appropriate to that particular trust**, both in terms of its declared policies and in the size of grant you ask for. Don't ask for £90,000 from a Trust whose largest grant is normally only £3,000 or which only has £3,000 to give away.

The application – specific details

Each application should include:

- A short general description of your organisation, stating who you are, how long you have been in business, what your main activities are and what some of your successes have been.
- Specific information about the nature and the size of the need, or the problem you are intending to address. Avoid at all costs such broad generalisations as 'addressing the needs of the elderly in Warminster', or, worse still, 'there is a desperate need for the service we plan to provide'.
- A specific description of the project or part of the organisation for which you are looking for funds.
- How you propose to tackle the need or problem, and clear and realistic objectives of what you are hoping to achieve.
- The cost of the project (or item) with, where necessary, a realistic, itemised budget for the work in question. It still amazes even hardened trust administrators when they receive applications that give no indication as to whether the cost in question is £5, £500, £5,000 or £500,000!
- The time-scale of the project: when you plan to start and how long the project will run – now, next year and over what period.
- Information as to whether other funders have been approached; are any applications under consideration, and have any grants been given?
- An indication, if a long-term project, of the possible sources of on-going funding after the grant-aid applied for has finished.

- Some indication of how you intend to monitor and evaluate your project (ie how will you measure success?).
- The latest set of accounts and an annual report. Bear in mind, however, that supporting material is not usually seen by the trustees.
- The name, status and telephone number of a contact person.
- Your registered charity number, of course.

Afterwards

In many activities in life, our eagerness to please beforehand changes, once gratified, to indifference or forgetfulness. It is important to acknowledge receipt of a grant and it may even be worth while saying 'Thank you'. You may want to re-apply to that particular trust in a year or two's time: whatever other qualities trust administrators may lack, they mostly have memories like the proverbial elephant.

Make a note of any requests or requirements for further information and ensure that you respond accordingly.

It is also worth keeping in touch, telling the grant giver about your progress, highlighting your successes, inviting them around to see your project on a special day or at a specific time. Building a relationship that is based upon respect on both sides is not possible with all trusts, but it is certainly worth while putting in the effort, especially for local and large funders. Trustees like to fund success: that is why they are in business. A satisfied trustee or administrator is more likely to want to consider further support.

The 'do nots' of applying

Do not:

- submit too much material or be too verbose – two pages should be the absolute maximum for most projects, unless you are asked for more;
- submit out-of-date material;
- use jargon (nobody but you will understand it);
- send a handwritten appeal (these are difficult to read);
- send a duplicated mailshot (straight in the waste-paper basket);
- answer questions on a standard application form with 'See attached';
- apply pressure by alluding to meetings or chance encounters with trustees 'who have encouraged me to write to you';
- end a letter with 'I would like this appeal to be taken seriously'(a guaranteed turn-off);
- respond to a rejection letter by sending an angry, rude or an insulting reply.

Some final thoughts

These may not be the pearls of wisdom that you had expected to drip from the collective silver pens of experienced grant makers. It is, perhaps you are saying, nothing but 'common sense'.

Fundraising is time consuming and hard work, requiring patience, tenacity and a dose of good fortune. Trusts, as stated at the start of this chapter, vary greatly, and there is no single formula that will guarantee success. Knowing what you want, being able to express that clearly and succinctly in writing, giving attention to detail and treating your trust or trusts as individual entities, not as a homogeneous mass, may increase your chances of success.

PART FOUR

Maintaining effective relationships

CHAPTER TEN

Acknowledgement, recognition and reporting

David Saint

Despatch of the completed application is far from the end of the fundraising process. If you are serious about securing a grant, rather than simply 'going through the motions', there is much more you can and should do to ensure success – this time or next.

It is important to bear in mind the fact that there *will be* a next time. One or two trusts almost always turn down the first application from a charity to see just how serious the charity is, and how it conducts itself. The steps you take once you have sent in your application could influence the decision about not just that grant, but also future ones.

Keeping track of progress

The way in which you record progress will depend upon how you normally do things – the system has to be comfortable or it will not be used. It should, however, contain three elements:

- First, a filing system will be essential, to enable you quickly to retrieve all the papers relating to a particular prospect as required.
- A simple checklist of all the necessary actions should be kept in the front of the file, with an indication of when they should be taken, and by whom.
- Finally, a diary function will be invaluable, to ensure that those actions are taken at the right time, without undue haste or panic.

It will be crucial to refer to the diary function on a daily basis (so it helps if this really is a diary) to ensure that the system works. It makes a lot more sense if the system is used for a large number of applications, or for other project management purposes as well, and the use of it becomes second nature.

Keeping trusts informed

Relationships are all about communication – but relevant communication. Trusts will generally welcome information about your project if it has a bearing on your application. Success in obtaining partial funding from a different source, a material alteration in the project team or the project itself, an award or achievement that reinforces your organisation's ability to deliver the project – all these things will be relevant to a potential funder, and should be brought to their attention. Simply bombarding them with newsletters and, worse still, direct-mail appeals will not be helpful.

Sometimes it will be sufficient to telephone the correspondent to advise them of the new information. In other circumstances a letter will suffice. If the change is significant, your application may have to be rewritten, or even withdrawn. Funders will generally respect an applicant who takes a responsible attitude to the information they supply. They may be less impressed by one who simply seems unable to make up his or her mind.

Following acknowledgement requirements

Many trusts have specific preferences when it comes to acknowledgement of grants. Some may wish to remain absolutely anonymous, perhaps because of their ethos of giving, or to avoid an avalanche of similar applications. It can be tempting to let the name slip, particularly in support of an application to another funder, but you should only do so with the express written permission of the donor.

Some trusts request an acknowledgement in the charity's Annual Report. If so, do not simply make the acknowledgement but remember also to send a copy to the donor, stating in the covering letter the page on which the acknowledgement can be found. Make sure (at proof stage!) that it has been spelled correctly.

Occasionally a trust will ask for a more overt acknowledgement, particularly in respect of larger grants. This might be anything from a plaque on a piece of furniture to the naming of a whole building. Discuss with the trust their precise requirements and their implications (for example the cost to the charity of providing the acknowledgement, or the feelings of other, perhaps more significant, donors). When these have been agreed, be sure they are implemented in good time and that the charity is invited to send a representative to see the project and the acknowledgement, or perhaps that they are sent a photograph of it.

Remember that trusts will expect any rules they may have (which may form part of their trust deed) to be followed. You may flout them once and get away with it. Any future application is very unlikely to be successful.

Thanking trusts and subsequent contact

Remember that trusts are administered by people. Thanking trusts needs to work at two, or possibly three, levels:

- The first level we have already considered – this is the public acknowledgement (or not) requested by the trust.
- The second level is the formal 'thank-you' letter. It should go without saying that one should be sent, but even this is frequently overlooked. Send one that is neither overly effusive nor a terse two-liner. The letter should be personal and addressed to the person who wrote the letter that accompanied the cheque (or, if there was not one, the person who signed the cheque), thanking the trust and the trustees for the grant of £XXX for project YY. It may be appropriate to add a little information on the project that did not appear in the original application, or to say something about the specific impact that the grant will have. It can also be worth mentioning in passing any other work you are doing that may be of interest to the trust in the future – but do not ask for a further grant at this stage!
- If there is an opportunity to go to the third level of thanks, this can be highly beneficial. The correspondent or one of the trustees may have been very helpful to you in the application process, or instrumental in securing a positive decision. Such input usually goes unnoticed and unacknowledged, especially if it is by a staff member, but expressing thanks person to person helps to build a real relationship which is not only good in its own right but also lays first-class foundations for subsequent application.

Reporting on progress

The process should not even end with your saying 'Thank you'. With the possible exception of smaller grants for one-off items, it can be very valuable to update trusts from time to time on the way your project is unfolding. This should not be in the form of junk mail (although update sheets that receive a wider circulation may be appropriate). The frequency of these reports might well be determined by any criteria set by the trust, the duration of the project and, perhaps, the absolute size of the grant. Updates should only be sent when there is some news (even if this is bad), and not so frequently that the trust is inundated with paper. A grant to cover a year's project might warrant two or three updates; a project of three months' duration might justify a report halfway through, and one at the end.

Keeping the trust involved

The staff and/or trustees of most trusts will simply not have the time to do anything much more than receive your reports – and perhaps only to skim-read those. Others, however, will take a more hands-on approach to their grant making and wish to become quite involved in the project. In the case of very substantial grants, they may want to have a nominee on the management committee or equivalent. In other cases, they may simply want to attend occasional meetings or visit the project from time to time. It is possible that the active involvement of a trust representative may be (or seem to be) unwelcome interference. It is more likely that other significant benefits will flow. The trust and its representative will be anxious to ensure that its grant is effective, and will wish to offer help and advice to ensure that the project succeeds. Their experience and expertise may complement your own; their contacts and influence may be very important to you. On the whole, the direct involvement of a trust representative can be highly beneficial and should be encouraged, if it seems possible.

Following up

You should follow up your applications in every circumstance, but the nature and timing of that follow up will vary from situation to situation and should have been identified at the point of application and recorded in your diary file (see Chapter 6 of this book). Here are seven different situations, which require different responses:

- **The trust informs you your project is outside its terms of reference**. If your research is at fault, there is not much you can do. A short courteous letter of apology for taking their time would not go amiss. If the published information suggests your project *should* be of interest to them, phone or write to request current guidelines, or to have them clarified if you already have them.
- **The trust advises you that its funds are fully committed**. If not revealed in the rest of the letter, phone or write to find out whether this will be the case for the foreseeable future and, if not, whether in principle your project is of interest and when you should reapply.
- **The trust invites you to reapply.** Do so, when they suggest, providing any further information they require.
- **The trust offers a grant but does not enclose the cheque.** Carry out any action they request, such as advising them when work on the project has begun. Make a diary note to do this if it cannot be done immediately. If a cheque does not arrive within a reasonable period of a grant being

approved (say four weeks) enquire politely whether it has been sent. Mistakes can happen – at either end!

- **The grant is received.** Acknowledge it, as outlined above. Read any accompanying material carefully, and ensure that you comply with any requirements stated within it. In the event that circumstances have changed so much that you will not be able to spend the grant on what you were given it for (perhaps the project is fully funded from elsewhere, or that precise activity is no longer needed), do not hesitate to return the cheque. Although this will be a painful thing to do after all the effort you went to to get it, you have a legal obligation to do this if you are not going to spend it as the donor expects. Of at least equal importance is the fact that this will earn you the considerable respect of the trust and may ease significantly every other dealing you ever have with them.
- **The period or project that a grant is to cover has elapsed.** By this time, the project will probably be very low on your list of priorities: it has been around a long time; other matters will have become more urgent or important; new initiatives will be clamouring for your fundraising attention. Do not be beguiled by them! Use your diary system to remind you to send a final report on the project to the trusts (and other major donors) that supported it – whether or not this was a condition of the grant. This is not only courteous, but also helps develop good relationships on which to found your next application.
- **A year has gone by.** Unless a trust states otherwise, it is generally felt that 12 months should elapse between one application and the next. Do not make this rigid, so that your applications become mechanistic and predictable, but do not assume that, if you have received one grant, you will be unlikely to be favoured again for some time. The reverse is often the case, especially if you have been sensible and conscientious in your acknowledgement, recognition and reporting.

CHAPTER ELEVEN

Consolidation

Roger Mitty

> The special thing about this job is that everyone is usually very nice to me – even when I have had to say 'No'. Most of them realise that I would much rather have said 'Yes'.

A senior administrator

Introduction

All fundraising methodologies, whether they involve companies, organisations or trusts, still involve people. Grants received by charities from grant-making trusts are essentially the result of people (in the form of trustees) responding to people (representing charitable organisations) and what they wish to provide for the community (people) they seek to serve.

It is important to understand that an application to a grant-making trust, whether that application has been successful or not, should not be seen as the end of a particular process. It should always be seen as either the beginning or the continuation of a potentially fruitful relationship between two organisations.

Information recording

Effective recording systems should and will play a vital part in supporting and driving the communications process through which a charity should consolidate its relationship with an individual trust. It is, therefore, very important that thorough and complete records are kept of the results of all the applications that your organisation makes to grant-making trusts, whether the outcome of that application has been successful or not.

This kind of information gathering is, of course, a continuous process and this data, a combination of both the initial and on-going research that a charity needs to carry out, will form the basis of an increasingly comprehensive database of information on all those trusts whose objects are in line with your particular cause. This information resource will become the single, most valuable asset to support the delivery of your researched and carefully phased strategy for fundraising from grant-making trusts and foundations.

Organisations are constantly evolving and changing. In the same way, charities will regularly re-appraise their priorities, the relevance of their work and ways in which they need to adapt to meet increasing or changing needs. In addition to the recording of all applications to trusts, all new projects and new areas of work need to be collated and recorded centrally. All areas of work should be regularly evaluated in terms of their relevance to the existing portfolio of trusts, the order of their urgency and their priority. There are other factors, such as working in new geographical areas, that will also affect the way a charity needs to adapt its fundraising strategy.

One of the single most important 'new developments' that will affect trust fundraising will be when a charity moves into a new area of operation beyond its traditional activities. It is almost certain that those changes will open up opportunities to consider an approach to a whole new tranche of trusts whose objects cover the new initiatives.

Contacts

As previous chapters have discussed, most people who are experienced in trust fundraising will appreciate that a charity should, if at all possible, get its application through any route except the letter box. The value of identifying and using personal contacts in developing an organisation's communications with grant-making trusts cannot be over-emphasised. The charity will need to have in place a research process under which the interests of any new committee members, trustees, friends and even supporters who become more closely involved and engaged with the charity and its work and vision are well recorded. There are countless experiences that demonstrate that, when a charity is able to make a personal contact with a trustee and create and encourage an opportunity for face-to-face conversations to encourage an interest in their organisation, the chances of a successful application are substantially increased. It is also the case that trust representatives are often more than willing to engage in conversations with charities considering an application. They appreciate and respond positively to organisations that have taken the time and the trouble to conduct quality research and investigation and speak intelligently about individual trusts to their representatives. That personal and individual contact also provides an opportunity for fundraisers to listen and hear what the trust is looking for. Sometimes, in their enthusiasm to grasp an opportunity to present the urgency of their cause, fundraisers are guilty of missing an opportunity to understand the prospective donor's views and needs. Whenever a representative of a charity has made personal contact with a trust representative, be that an administrator or trustee, there should be a full de-brief of that individual in order that soft information can be gathered to support the application process.

A note on timing

Application intervals

Understandably, many grant-making trusts will only accept an application from an individual charity once a year. Some trusts specifically state when the next application might be made, and occasionally charities may be able to approach a particular trust more than once in an individual year if there is a special one-off or urgent need. Conversely, others require a three-year, or even longer, interval between applications and therefore wish to be only occasional supporters. Charities will consequently need to monitor application intervals on individual trusts on a regular basis. This is much easier if the charity is engaging in a structured communications process and relationship-building activity rather than simply sending applications will-nilly through the post. It is worth remembering that this policy may also change as a trust grows, shrinks or appoints different administrative or trustee personnel.

Lead times

Trusts vary tremendously in the time they allow to elapse between a charity's submission of an application for a grant and the trustees' final consideration of that application, and also in the process by which they inform the charity. These lead times may range from a few weeks for some smaller trusts to over a year for the much larger trusts. It is the fundraiser's responsibility to research and understand that process on an individual trust basis. It is also a fundraiser's responsibility to keep their organisation informed of these processes. Charities are ever conscious of cashflow, but, if senior representatives of the charity expect that an application to a trust means a response and money in the bank within weeks, they are being unrealistic!

Evaluating success

A great deal can be learned from careful evaluation of the success of presenting different types of projects or engaging in different styles of approach to grant-making trusts, and it is important to monitor charities' success in meeting financial targets for trust fundraising. Keeping careful track of responses from trusts to other charities in terms of the levels of success and grant gifts may give a valuable insight into your charity's own success.

There is every indication that the fundraising environment will continue to become increasingly competitive. Like most organisations, charities and not-for-profit organisations are constantly changing. Charities introduce new projects, new services, expand into new geographical areas. There are also constant changes in how trusts operate and how trustees address the not inconsiderable responsibility of distributing their funds. Every month new trusts are established. Sometimes these new trusts are unhappy to advertise their presence widely for fear of being overwhelmed by fundraising organisations. Always fundraisers need to ensure that they are doing all that is reasonably possible to identify those changes, recognise new opportunities and adapt approaches to optimise success rates.

Summary

Good planning and research are essential to trust-fundraising success. The results experienced by successful trust fundraisers clearly demonstrate that the extra efforts applied to planning, organising and consolidating in the ways described in this book are well worth while, even for the smallest of charities. It is disappointing that so many fundraising organisations are still not prepared to invest sufficiently in a strategic and phased approach to trust fundraising that could attract a steady stream of income to their cause and continue to make billions of pounds available to the charity sector.

In consolidating their fundraising approaches, at the very least charities should always:

- record results;
- report regularly, appropriately and personally to trusts on the progress of projects that those trusts have supported and, indeed, other projects that fall within their area of interest;
- develop a regular programme of contact, including visits by trust representatives to projects;
- continue a process of research on existing and new trusts;
- carefully monitor lead times for applications;
- regularly evaluate relative success across projects and application styles;
- report to the organisation as a whole, including volunteer contacts, on the results of applications;
- co-ordinate trust fundraising activity with other fundraising efforts;
- frequently analyse research and look for new opportunities.

CHAPTER **TWELVE**

Recording systems

Peter Flory

Introduction

If you are going to use computers to help you monitor the process of fundraising from trusts and to carry out some of the mundane tasks involved, then you must ensure that you record the right data at the right time, have fast and efficient access to the data when you need it and that you are able to produce letters and analysis reports at any time. The first thing to consider is what system to choose.

Types of system available

There are three types of systems to consider.

The new range of Information Directories available on CD-ROM

These are invaluable sources of readily available information on trusts and they can even do some of the things one would normally associate with a contact database. You can select a number of trusts in which you are interested, link them to your favourite word-processing system and produce a mail-merged letter to them all (not a process that is recommended in trust fundraising). However, these CD-ROMs are not the focus of this part of the book and they are best used in conjunction with a contact database to provide the starting point for the application process.

A do-it-yourself database – for example using Microsoft's Access software

You can create a system using Access or a similar database development tool. This will give you exactly what you want and you can take the data defined later in this chapter as a starting point.

***One of the many packaged Contact Database/Fundraising systems
on the market***

There are at least 60 of these available, but it is fair to say that there are about
a dozen market leaders, for example Raiser's Edge or Alms. Most of these systems will have facilities required to monitor the application process.

Major data recording requirements

To manage and monitor your fundraising from trusts you will need to maintain information of the following general type:

- all identified trusts
- those trusts thoughtfully discounted, with reasons
- history of giving
- history of relationships
- all productive relationships
- records of contacts
- records of applications, successes, failures, rejections, with reasons
- timespans for future actions, including built-in prompts.

Key functions to be performed

All of the functions required on trust data are what you would expect of any
contact database. These include the ability to:

- add and amend trust records easily and make maximum use of techniques
  like picking items from drop-down lists (eg giving policy, action types, etc);
- add and amend applications just as easily;
- add and amend details of mailings to/other communications with the trust
  just as easily;
- link all trustees and other people you know at the trust to the trust record;
- select trust records to view on screen immediately by inputting one or a
  combination of data items (eg trust name, trustee name, postcode or other
  elements of the address, geographic area served, particular giving policy,
  etc);
- carry out complex selections for mailing (eg all trusts that haven't given
  before and that are based in the south-east, or all trusts that have a trustee
  who is also a personal donor to the charity);
- use output of selections to produce mail-merged letters or labels via a link
  with Word, WordPerfect or Wordpro and to produce Mailing History
  records;
- perform diary management including an automatic reminder on due dates;
- record *ad-hoc* letters, telephone calls, etc;

- record grants received and maintain every income item that comes in against the respective trust but also summary information for every trust (eg the size of the first and last gift, the largest gift, the average gift value, the lifetime gift value and the total number of gifts);
- run, as and when required, a set of standard reports, including number and value of applications made, awards received and success rate, specified time periods for applications that have been exceeded, and also amounts received year-to-date compared with budget;
- carry out variable analyses of applications and income (eg the use of an easy-to-use report writer);
- import names and addresses to the database;
- export data to other systems (eg to spreadsheets, for further analysis and the production of graphical output).

Key data to be recorded

In order to carry out the functions above, you will need to record data of the following types:

- basic trust details (including their giving policy and procedures)
- trustees and other contacts
- past and future actions
- applications made
- grants received
- thank-you and other letters and general mailing history
- log of other communications
- funds/projects for which you need funds
- ad-hoc notes.

Basic trust details

There are two types of information required here: the standard contact data needed on any fundraising source, and the specific data required on trusts.

Standard data

- trust name
- address with separately identifiable fields for address lines, town, county and postcode
- telephone/fax numbers
- name and job title of main mailing contact
- list of the types of mailings they should receive.

Specific data for trusts

- giving policy (what things they give to, what things they don't give to, which areas of the country/world they support or don't support, with what frequency they will consider applications – eg 'don't apply again for three years', etc)
- application procedures
- when to apply, meeting dates and decision timetable
- total annual grants awarded for the last three years
- largest known single award
- average award
- who else they give to.

Trustees and other contacts

It is also essential to record details of individuals on the database and link them to any trusts or trustees they may know (with a two-way link) so that when viewing the trust record you can see a list of people and their relationship to the trust (eg trustee, chief executive, administrator) and, conversely, when viewing an individual's record you can see the organisations (and other people) with whom they have a relationship, and the nature of that relationship.

Past and future actions

This is a simple record consisting of date, action type (ie telephone call, letter, etc), who created the action, to whom the action is assigned and an action summary/comment. An extremely useful feature here allows for future dates to be entered and actions automatically displayed on the computer screen on the appropriate day to remind you (or the person to whom you have assigned the action) what you have to do today or this week.

Applications made

The application may be a simple letter or a complex proposal, but it is important to record the basics of each application, such as:

- trust
- application date
- amount applied for
- what it was for (fund/project code)
- who is dealing with it
- status of the application
- a space for the amount awarded (and an automatic calculation of the award as a percentage of the application).

Grants received

When an award is made, it is vital to record the amount received on the same record as the amount applied for, in order to carry out analysis. You may also have a standard format for recording all fundraising income, so the amount received must be recorded here as well. This income record usually consists of:

- date
- supporter donor (ie the trust in this case) number
- amount
- campaign/appeal code (often a general code for trust applications)
- fund/project code (what the application was for)
- payment type
- payment method
- receipt indicator.

'Thank-you' and other letters

This record, created whenever any correspondence is sent to the trust, consists of Date, Letter type, Who sent/signed it, a Comment, and Campaign/Appeal and Fund codes, if relevant. It should also ideally have a link to the actual text of the letter. The concept can be extended to letters coming into your organisation as well. Some charities now scan these incoming letters and then link the scanned image to the trust with a record similar to that outlined above.

Log of other communications

It helps to have a complete picture of all contacts with a trust and details of other communications with them (eg telephone calls – in and out, faxes, e-mails, meetings with them, events, etc and details of trustees or trust staff invited to attend). These could all be included in a single Communication/Activity log with the letter details above.

Funds/projects

In its simplest form, this records, for every fund/project for which money is being sought, a Fund Code, Description, Amount required, Amount received to date (which should be updated automatically as money is received).

Ad-hoc notes

There will always be things that should be recorded about a trust that do not fit into neat compartments. So an unlimited Notepad is an essential item.

Basic data requirements

- All identified trusts
- Those thoughtfully discounted, with reasons
- History of giving
- History of relationships
- Records of contacts
- Records of applications, successes, failures, rejections – with reasons
- Timespans for future action
- Built-in prompts
- All productive relationships

Why do systems fail?

Systems that should help trust fundraisers sometimes fail to live up to their expectations and fall into disuse for a number of well-documented reasons. These include:

- The system is unfriendly and difficult to use. There are still a large number of character-based, rather than Windows-based, systems around. Windows systems are more intuitive and therefore easier to use.
- The data can be entered into the system, but reporting it is difficult, often to the extent that it is actually impossible to obtain the reports needed.
- Inappropriate software – the system doesn't actually do what you want it to do. In other words, it was specified incorrectly in the first place.
- The system is inefficient and time consuming. No one is going to use a system with which it takes longer to change a record and link to word processing to print letters or labels than it does to amend an index card and type letters or labels on a typewriter.
- Some systems are inflexible. Once the basic tables are set up they cannot be altered by users. Fundraising changes, and flexibility is important. Neither the time nor the money is available to get IT people to change the system.
- Users do not keep the systems up to date (often because the systems are so difficult to use). There is no point in entering all the trustees for a trust and linking all the records together if it is not possible to keep up with changes and link new trustees and unlink ex-trustees, as the changes occur.
- The wrong details are recorded or the system does not allow the necessary data to be recorded. This can lead to applications for the wrong things (eg

asking for money for projects that the trust does not support) or for inappropriate amounts (eg for £50,000 when the maximum grant is £5,000) or at the wrong time (eg applying in December when the trust allocates its grants in November).

- Many systems are simply reactive data recorders rather than proactive tools to help the fundraising process. Recording historic actions is reactive, but recording future actions and having the computer produce reminders on the appropriate day is proactive. A good system needs both.
- Some systems link to word processing in order to send letters but they do not automatically create a mailing history record, so at a later date it is not possible to find out what was sent to whom.

Avoiding failure

There are some golden rules to follow when selecting any piece of software in order to avoid installing an inappropriate system:

- Set your objectives and be sure of what you are trying to achieve by installing the system.
- Define your requirements carefully and get the agreement of all interested parties.
- Allocate priorities to requirements – no system will do everything you can think of.
- Define selection criteria so that you have a benchmark for the comparison of competing systems.
- Check suppliers carefully, see demonstrations and take up references.
- Ensure that someone in your organisation understands the technical issues and can solve minor problems.

Finally, if you follow these golden rules when the system is in operation, you stand a good chance of avoiding disappointment:

- Update the data in the system continuously.
- Ensure all data in the system is accurate – remember, GIGO (garbage in, garbage out)!
- Record relevant data.
- Always set review dates.
- Track trustee movements.
- Record trustee interests.

PART FIVE

Additional perspectives

CHAPTER THIRTEEN

The trusts' perspective

Nigel Siederer, Chief Executive, Association of Charitable Foundations

Introduction

The following is an extract from the Association of Charitable Foundations' (ACF's) 1998 advisory leaflet, 'Applying to a Charitable Trust or Foundation', which has been reproduced with the ACF's permission.

The size of the sector

There are about 8,800 grant-making trusts and foundations in the UK, giving in total about £1.25 billion per year to charitable causes. To this might be added £320 million given by the National Lottery Charities Board and £280 million given by a dozen large operating charities, such as Imperial Cancer Research and Oxfam, that make grants in the course of their work, making £1.85 billion in all.

Total grant giving to the voluntary sector by trusts is about the same as that of central or local government (excluding government grants to housing associations and employment schemes), and larger than that of the corporate sector. The figures are, however, notoriously difficult to analyse, and are complicated by the 'contract culture', so comparisons can be misleading. For example, although government gives little grant aid to voluntary organisations in the educational field, its total spending on education is about £31 billion, whereas trust spending is £320 million. Similar comparisons emerge in social welfare. This is why trusts fight shy of long-term funding of services, especially services that could reasonably be part of state provision. However, in some fields, such as medical research, trust funding can be quite significant.

What trusts fund

Trusts can preserve their distinctive role only by doing special things. They therefore like to concentrate their funding on:

- new methods of tackling problems;
- disadvantaged and minority groups that have trouble using ordinary services, or that are inadequately served by them;
- responses to new or newly discovered needs and problems;
- work that is hard to finance through conventional fundraising;
- one-off purchases or projects, including research;
- short- and medium-term work that is likely to bring a long-term benefit and/or to attract long-term funding from elsewhere.

Core funding is not ruled out for work that falls into one or more of these categories.

Selecting trusts

Use the various directories to locate trusts that may be able to help – and to rule out those that will not be interested. Draw up a shortlist of possible trusts. Your list should include:

- Trusts that operate in your geographical area. Look especially for any trusts that can *only* fund in your area or that express a preference for it. Don't approach a trust that *cannot* fund in your area, nor ask for funding for a national project from a trust that is limited to a particular locality. A trust that funds nationally may be interested in a local project if it particularly matches the trust's interests and/or is of national significance (ie it would make a grant because of the pioneering nature of the project's work rather than because of the needs of the area). Only the very largest national trusts (the top 50 or so) are able to fund local projects more widely than this.
- Trusts that are interested in your field of work and the sort of people who will benefit from it. If a trust says that it makes grants only in a particular field or to benefit a particular age group, it means it. Likewise, if a trust says that it does not fund general appeals, or that projects of a particular type are excluded, don't try to persuade it that you are the exception.
- Trusts that make (and have sufficient funds to make) grants of the size you need. Don't ask a small trust for too much (or a large one for too little).

Many trusts publish information leaflets for applicants (this is often reproduced in the various directories or may be downloaded from trusts' websites, many of which may be reached via ACF's site at www.acf.org.uk/foundations).

Write off for, or download, these details, and use them to refine your shortlist, which will usually be quite short – perhaps only three or four trusts, and probably not more than twenty. Where a trust's information says that it has an application form, obtain this before proceeding further; don't waste time drafting a letter until you have completed the form. Most trusts, however, do not use an application form.

If you can't find any trusts that seem likely to be interested, think again about how to present your work. Can you describe it in a different way, emphasising different (and preferably unusual) aspects that may attract a different group of funders? If the amount of money you need is too large, can you sub-divide the proposal into smaller projects?

Writing your application

Remember to include the following points:

- The purpose of the work to be funded – who it will help and how, what is distinctive about it, what will be achieved if a grant is given (and perhaps what will not be achieved if a grant is not given).
- A budget for the project. Work out your needs carefully. Don't economise on essentials, such as training or unavoidable overhead costs.
- Ask for a specific sum of money. If necessary, say that you are seeking a contribution of £X towards a total budget of £Y, and that you hope to raise the remainder from other sources, which you specify. Do not simply say that you are a very worthwhile organisation and desperately need funds.
- Your name, address, and phone number – oh yes, people do forget!

Make the application long enough to describe what you want properly, but short enough for it to be easy to take in at first reading – usually no more than two pages for your main letter.

Don't overload the application with attachments. A trust that is seriously interested will ask for anything it hasn't got. You should, however, always include your most recent annual report and accounts. (If your accounts show apparently large reserves, attach a note explaining why you hold them and why they cannot be used to fund the project for which you are seeking funds. If you cannot explain the size of your reserves, consider spending them, instead of applying for grants!)

If your organisation does not have charitable status, explain why the work to be funded is charitable, and if possible name a registered charity that will take responsibility for any grant on your behalf (providing written confirmation from that charity). You *must* identify such a charity when applying to a trust that has a policy of funding only registered charities.

How do trusts spend their money?

Preferred timescale

1 year or less	24%
Up to three years	24%
More than three years	8%
Unspecified	44%

Capital/revenue/project

One-off grants, projects and feasibility studies	86%
Running or recurring costs including salaries	18%
Capital other than buildings	17%
Core costs	13%
Buildings	12%

Preferred fields of grant-making

Social care and development	35%
Health	33%
Arts, culture and recreation	31%
Accommodation and housing	24%
Conservation and environment	23%
Religious activities	22%
Infra-structure	17%

Source Pharoah (1997)

Connecting with trusts

Apply well before you need the money. Trusts generally make decisions through trustees' meetings which take place every two or three months. Some meet only two or three times a year. While a few trusts have small grants programmes where a fast response can be given, most are unable to deal quickly even with the very best applications.

Trusts generally have quite limited administrative capacity. Although the largest trusts are quite substantial organisations, only the top 300 or so employ any staff at all. The vast majority of trusts are run on a part-time or voluntary basis, and are themselves very small organisations. Don't expect too much of them. The sheer volume of applications means that most trusts do not normally acknowledge applications, and many are unable to reply to applicants who are ultimately unsuccessful. If you want to be sure of an acknowledgement, send a reply-paid postcard addressed to yourself.

Many trusts visit at least the larger applications they are considering. If you receive a visit, it is usually a sign that you have got over the first hurdle. Try to establish what the funder wishes to see and who they wish to meet. It is useful also to identify how long the funder can spend with you. Are they hoping to see your project in action, as well as discuss the organisation's work? Are they interested in the whole organisation or just this particular project? The answers to these questions will help you decide which of you should be there.

What trusts look for

Trusts usually make visits in order to assess the need for the project and the extent to which the applicants have come up with a good solution. They will also be looking for reassurance that the applicants are able to deliver what they promise. This is your chance to bring the project to life, so try to ensure that the person meeting the funder both knows about the project and is enthusiastic about it.

While some trusts will want to visit you, others will deal with your application entirely by letter. Some will be willing to discuss the application (or a prospective application) over the phone, while others will not. (If a trust's directory entry does not include a phone number, this means that phone calls are unwelcome. It will not help you to trace the number through Directory Enquiries.)

If you happen to know a trustee of a trust, tell him or her that you are applying. But in general it won't help you to approach trustees direct; deal with a trust through its designated secretary or correspondent.

Remember that trusts get many more applications than they can fund. A typical trust, if there is such a thing, may be able to fund only one in four of the eligible applications received, and half or more of the enquiries it receives may be ineligible. So if you don't succeed, it may not reflect on the quality of your application. The reasons that applications may be ineligible are that they are outside the trust's stated guidelines, or lack obvious details such as a return address.

If you are lucky enough to receive a grant, ensure first of all that you acknowledge receipt of the cheque and thank the funder – it is surprising how many applicants do not do this.

Three golden rules

Trusts vary enormously in their policies, styles of working, and administrative capacities.

- Do your homework beforehand.
- Prepare your application carefully.
- Leave plenty of time.

CHAPTER **FOURTEEN**

The American perspective

David Wickert

Why should US foundations bother with the UK?

Why should a foundation in the USA fund a charity in the UK? We know that UK charities do get US funding, but why?

It is sometimes as a result of personal contact. One of your trustees or volunteers or clients is an American or knows an American who is on the board of a US foundation, and with their encouragement the foundation offers your charity a grant.

Or there is an overlap of interests. A US company, through its associated foundation in the UK, sees a chance to enhance its profile in your community, where it has customers, suppliers and employees, by supporting your organisation.

Or your charity does work in a third country, work not done by any US non-profit-organisation. Because your application enthuses a US foundation, it supports the work that you are doing. It may already support similar work in other parts of the world undertaken by other charities outside the USA.

There are numerous similar scenarios. The US foundation sector is very large and it supports an enormous range of charitable activity. Board members of US foundations and the professional managers they employ are always on the look out for projects that fit their foundations' giving interests. Of course, most are looking in the US, but suitable projects are to be found all over the world, including the UK. And foundations depend, at least in part, on the best projects being brought to their attention by grant applicants.

Like UK grant-making trusts, most US foundations were established to support a particular community, or local cause. A substantial proportion of US foundations will not accept unsolicited applications – these are of no direct interest to UK fundraisers.

Several hundred foundations do, however, make grants to support charities outside the US and they publish information to assist non-American charities to make applications (the American Express Foundation and the Ford Foundation, for example, are both well known and very large). There are even foundations that make grants only outside the US (eg Christopher Reynolds Foundation, China Medical Board of New York, Central European University Foundation), but they are rare.

There are several hundred more that do not advertise the fact but that are prepared to make an international grant if they receive a particularly appropriate application.

In 1996 the US foundation sector made grants in excess of $22 billion (nearly £14 billion). Grants to support causes outside the US totalled nearly $2 billion, and every indication is that this figure is rising faster than other giving. However, set against the total giving of individual Americans ($109 billion), it is still modest.

The structure of the US charitable sector

There are many delightful similarities between UK grant-making trusts and US foundations. This chapter will highlight these similarities and explain the significance of the differences.

There are considerable similarities between the structure of the UK and US charitable sectors. In the US the philanthropic sector is, very broadly, divided into two parts: public charities and private foundations. These are similar to fundraising charities and grant-making trusts in the UK. In both cases, the first group offers services, and the second group makes grants to fund the services offered. However, the laws that regulate them in the US are very different from charity law in the UK.

In the US, Public Charities and Private Foundations are both 501(c)(3)s. Section 501(c)(3) is a part of the US Internal Revenue Code that refers to charities. Public Charities are usually called 'nonprofits' (often '501(c)(3)s', particularly in written material you may see from foundations), which is how they are referred to in this chapter. Private foundations will be called 'foundations'.

Charitable tax arrangements in the US

US nonprofits are funded by donations from the public, and by grants from foundations. Foundations are funded by an individual, a small group of individuals, a family or a company. The funders often provide a substantial endowment.

To understand how foundations operate it is necessary to know the major differences between the UK and the US tax systems as they relate to charitable giving.

In the US there is no tax reclaim, therefore no covenants or Gift Aid. There is a different tax mechanism to achieve what is called in the UK 'tax efficiency'. This mechanism is called an income-tax deduction.

When a US individual or company gives a gift to a nonprofit or endows a foundation, they take an income-tax deduction. This means that their gross taxable income is reduced, dollar by dollar, by the amount that they have given. They are therefore not taxed on what they gave and, because there is a reduction in their tax liability, a deduction is perceived in the US as a benefit to the donor. This is unlike the UK where tax reclaim is seen as a benefit to the charity that gets the reclaimed tax.

It is very straightforward for a US individual or company to get this tax deduction. It just means entering the gift on the annual tax return (and all US taxpayers must complete a return every year). Therefore, a deduction is taken for virtually every gift to a nonprofit or a foundation.

Importantly for the purposes of this chapter, no deduction can be taken for a gift made to a charity outside the USA. This does not prevent cheques being written directly to charitable organisations outside the US, nor is there anything improper about it, but the absence of a tax deduction does make doing such a thing most untypically American.

Those who endow a foundation take a tax deduction when they make the gift. Then the foundation must by law give away 5 per cent of its capital each year. This does not mean that they will all cease to exist in 20 years time – income from new endowments and investments may far exceed 5 per cent – but it is good news for grant seekers that the foundation *has* to give money away.

Not only must foundations give 5 per cent away, but they can only give to nonprofits, or to organisations outside the US that can be demonstrated to be organised and operated in a way equivalent to a US nonprofit. There are several ways in which a foundation can establish that a non-US organisation fulfils this equivalency rule, but it is enough of a legal hurdle to deter many foundations from making any international grants.

American friends

Given this state of affairs, it would seem a good idea for charities outside the USA to make it easier for foundations to give them money, and there are several ways of doing this.

The first is for the charity to set up its own nonprofit. These nonprofits are often (but not always, there is no rule about it) called 'The American Friends of' (for example, The American Friends of Oxford University). This chapter describes these nonprofits as American Friends, even though this is not what they are always called – the American Friends of The National Trust, for example, is called the Royal Oak Foundation.

American Friends are not (in the vast majority of cases) 'wholly owned subsidiaries' of the UK charity; they are independent American organisations, and they have to be run as independent organisations with independent US trustees, usually called in the US the Board of Directors. Under US law, the Board of Directors of an American Friends needs to take real decisions about grants to the UK charity. If the grants are made 'automatically' without a Board decision, there is always the danger that the US Internal Revenue Service (IRS) will consider that the American Friends is acting merely as a conduit, and will expect a foundation that makes a grant to exercise equivalency regarding the eventual charitable recipient in the UK.

As the name may suggest, American Friends have another very significant role, which is that individual American taxpayers can take a deduction when they make a gift. This is particularly useful for organisations, such as UK universities, that have graduates in the US who couldn't get a deduction if they gave directly to the university in the UK.

An alternative to American Friends is the nonprofits that have been set up wholly or in part as intermediary organisations to facilitate grants to charities outside the US. The terms on which they do this will vary. They include Charities Aid Foundation America, the American Fund for Charities, and the British Schools and Universities Foundation. They act as American Friends of 'friendless' charities outside the US (for contact details see 'Useful organisations', p 136).

Other UK charities have developed close reciprocal links with a nonprofit, often one doing similar work, which will handle grants for them.

Without an American Friends of your own, or a friendly intermediary nonprofit, some foundations will not fund you, because you are outside the USA. This important preparation for US grant seeking is a result of the US charitable tax law. Nothing similar is required in the UK unless you are recruited by a US nonprofit seeking funds from a UK grant-making trust!

Researching US charitable activity

Unless you already have up-to-date information to hand, you should research your particular area of activity in the US philanthropic sector.

You need to ensure that your charity, its projects and programmes are attractive to potential funding foundations. They are looking for interesting, innovative, cost-effective, measurable and preferably replicable projects that are within your charity's capacity to deliver.

There are many ways of doing this research – consultancy, networking, desk research, US publications, the Internet – all of which will also familiarise you to some extent with American terminology, including some of the technical and legal terminology that is dealt with in this chapter.

You need to have done enough research to be able to present your project in the most effective way, emphasising those elements that are most likely to be of interest to a funder.

Foundation research

The next step is to obtain information about foundations. This can be found in directories, the most widely used of which in the US are published by the Foundation Center (see pp 130 and 139). The Foundation Center also makes a great deal of its foundation material available on CD-ROM and on the Internet. Foundation Center publications contain huge quantities of material, but it is presented in American for Americans – for example, information is presented by state, which makes perfect sense if you are in America and naturally looking locally in the first place, but is less useful if you are looking right across all the states for foundations that will fund you in the UK.

However, because your research is focused on foundations that will make international grants, you have the option of using specialist publications: Chapel & York Directories, for example, are designed specifically for charities outside the USA (Chapel & York's UK address is given on page 137; details of publications are to be found on p 131).

Many charities get clues from other charities, or from their trustees, of foundations that it would be worth investigating. It really is worth trying to pin these rumours down and get the name of the foundation exactly correct. Sometimes there are (literally) hundreds of foundations whose titles contain the same familiar name.

If you have the opportunity, it is good to look at a variety of directories to decide which suits you the best (see 'Useful publications and other sources of information', p 123). You will have to depend upon their indexes to identify foundations that are interested, in principal, in supporting projects like yours. You are, in the first place, looking for foundations that say that they give to charities outside the US, but it is not unreasonable to consider foundations that do give nationally throughout the USA and whose objects fit very closely indeed with your funding requirements.

You may also want to consider a foundation if it supports only what you want to fund even though it does not mention funding outside the US, or if it only supports US nonprofits working in a particular country, which is where you work. There is, however, no point whatsoever in communicating with foundations that only give in a particular state or city in the US or that do not accept unsolicited applications.

Grant-making guidelines

Whatever you discover in a directory, no matter how encouraging and interesting, it cannot give you all the information you require. Directories can only be as good as the material on which they are based, and the directory entry is at best a summary of what the foundation supplies about itself. Because foundations can change almost every aspect of their operation at the drop of a hat, from their address right through to what they will fund, the solution is to do nothing until you have obtained the 'grant-making guidelines' of a foundation you are interested in.

Most foundations that accept unsolicited applications produce guidelines, which vary from a single duplicated page to a substantial little book. Your reason for obtaining these guidelines is to see what the foundation says about itself in its own words, to discover as exactly as possible what it will fund, and to find out the form in which an application for funds must be made. These guidelines are similar in their purpose to applications for statutory funding in the UK.

These guidelines are vital (without them you may spoil your chances by submitting something inadequate or irrelevant), and you can obtain them by telephoning, faxing or e-mailing, or by writing. But a word of warning: say as little as you can about your organisation in order to prevent someone at the foundation saying 'We do not fund that' or 'We do not fund outside the US' and hanging up. Say only that you are wanting the guidelines so that you can decide whether to make an application (true, after all). If questioned about your wanting funds outside the US say that the funds are to go to a 501(c)(3) (also true) but that you would prefer not to say more until you have seen the guidelines.

Increasingly, foundations are putting their guidelines on the Internet. A reasonably comprehensive list of the available private and company foundations guidelines can be found at www.fdncenter.org.

If possible, use a US address for the guidelines to be mailed to: it may be difficult to persuade any but the very largest foundations to mail guidelines outside the US. If when you telephone you get an answering machine, dictate your address very slowly and clearly indeed. Accents on the telephone are funny things!

When you receive the guidelines (and, no matter how hard you try and how creative you are, there are some you will never receive) see if they live up to your directory-based expectations. If they are unsuitable, forget it. If they are all you ever wanted, prepare an application.

Preparing your application

Prepare your application by providing the foundation with exactly what the guidelines stipulate, neither more nor less. If there is something that you cannot provide you must say why. Translate figures into dollars, but keep figures in sterling alongside (in brackets) for reference. Add international dialling codes to telephone and fax numbers – in fact, do everything and anything to make the application as easy to understand as possible.

It is at this point that assistance from an American can be invaluable, although only someone with experience of nonprofits will be able to translate the technical language that may come up. If you have any questions about what items in the guidelines mean, ask an American; even more importantly, ask an American to read your completed application and to identify any words or phrases that will be incomprehensible in the USA, or mean something completely different: 'this scheme', for example, will have bad associations (connected with 'scheming') for an American.

One thing that the guidelines will not tell you is how much money to apply for. This is obviously a very significant decision, particularly when you are making an application to a wealthy foundation and the sky's the limit. Some directories will give you an indication of the total value and number of grants made in a recent year, and you may be able to extrapolate an appropriate figure to ask for. These figures in a directory will also enable you to ask for a realistic figure from a small foundation. As in the UK, it is generally necessary to give a figure. You will, of course, usually be asked to say what has already been raised and promised.

Unless the guidelines say otherwise, you can telephone with any questions that you cannot resolve in any other way. Foundation officers may well be prepared to answer more questions than they would for an American down the road, because of your rarity value.

Sending your application

When you are satisfied that your application is ready, it is almost always better to post it than to fax it. Some foundations specify the form in which they will accept applications: do as they say. This means leaving sufficient time for your application to reach its destination by any deadline the foundation has imposed. If you are cutting it fine, an international delivery service like DHL may save a day or two, but they cost a good deal more. They do, however, provide confirmation that your application has arrived.

Some foundations will acknowledge applications; most will not; some you will only hear from if your application is successful. If you are successful, bless the day you read this chapter, and telephone the foundation to thank them. Ask if they know other foundations that might also consider funding your projects. The foundation world is a small world when it comes to things like this. Say 'thank you' in writing as well and, of course, fulfil to the letter all the reporting requirements regarding your use of the grant.

Follow-up activity

If you are unsuccessful, and the foundation has not explained their reasons for rejecting you, telephone and ask why they didn't fund you and whether they know of any other foundation that might consider funding your project. They may think your project is great but just not have the funding available.

When you make an application to another foundation you will have to be careful to rewrite anything you have prepared previously that is not exactly right. Be prepared to discard anything that is suspect. Provide exactly what the guidelines ask.

Conclusion

Contrary to what was said at the beginning of this chapter about not relying primarily on luck, there are some fundraisers who say that they simply started telephoning US foundations and within half an hour had a firm commitment, followed, two days later, by a hand-delivered cheque for a vast sum. These stories are very encouraging – but if they don't happen for you, return to the beginning of this chapter and start the process again, step by step.

In conclusion

Anthony Clay

Introduction

In the 1997 edition of CAF's *Dimensions of the Voluntary Sector,* Cathy Pharoah and Nigel Siederer constructed a number of valuable estimates of charitable grant making in the UK. These showed:

- charitable grant-making is considerably greater than previous work had indicated;
- although the income of these trusts is substantially derived from investments, about a quarter of grant makers have income from other sources;
- grant making by CAF's top 500 trusts grew by 5.4 per cent in real terms in 1996, even excluding the National Lottery Charities Board (NLCB).

The overall picture may not be one of dramatic change (in 1997, on average the amount of grant making did not change much from the previous year), but there is, in fact, considerable movement in the fortunes and activities of trusts. From time to time new trusts emerge, either through mergers (eg Lloyds TSB Foundation), events (eg the Diana, Princess of Wales Memorial Fund) or government initiatives (eg the NLCB). From time to time they shrink dramatically for special reasons (eg the Baring Foundation).

How should grant makers react to change?

Sometimes change has a very major effect on the grant makers. Consider, for example, the situation of a trust that typically supports a range of causes including the arts, medical research, welfare and heritage. The arrival of National Lottery grant-making bodies for heritage, the arts, charities and the millennium – often with a requirement that matching or partnership funds should be raised – has made a dramatic difference to the nature of requests. Combine this with the growth in new charities, especially NHS trusts, the establishment of a 'contract culture' where charities increasingly compete for business with the private sector, and the sharp decline in statutory funding, and we can see why the larger grant-making trusts are increasingly feeling that others are trying to write their agendas for them. Should a trust favour lottery-funded projects or not? Should it fund a service-providing charity when this may simply have the effect of enabling that charity to undercut a commercial supplier? How far should the trust be prepared to replace what was previously state funded? Should the trust change its policies in response to the arrival of huge new grant makers?

These are very real dilemmas, which have meant that grant-making trusts are constantly reviewing the situation and changing their policies. In consequence CAF's *Directory of Grant Making Trusts*, and DSC's *Guide to the Major Trusts* (and their associated CD-Roms) are becoming rapidly out of date, and the work of grant seekers is becoming harder.

Most grant makers report remarkable increases in the number of requests they receive. Much of this can be put down to the growth in availability of word processors that allow for rapid mass mailing of applications. Sometimes media publicity will attract a flood of new requests. Sometimes the upsurge in demand is the result of increasing professionalism in charities that had not previously taken trust fundraising very seriously.

All these pressures are making grant makers think hard about how they process enquiries and indeed, in some cases, whether they can process them at all. Some may, therefore, look nervously at the arrival of this new book, for fear that it may have the effect of stimulating more and more pressure.

It is to be hoped that this will not be the case. Time and again the authors of these pages have been urging research and focus, so that fewer trusts may be approached for irrelevant causes and, more often than before, applications will be highly relevant to the grant maker's objects and policies. After all, trust administrators have been as likely to complain of a shortage of good projects for funding as of there being too many.

The responsibilities of grant seekers

Grant seekers have a duty to do their homework and get to know the grant makers and what they are looking for. In turn the grant makers are becoming increasingly proactive, in some cases even creating their own projects for funding and asking very searching questions of the charities to which they grant.

In a recent case, a charity seeking a huge 'lead gift' from a trust was refused such a large amount until it had satisfied the grant makers that it had done all that it could to secure the support of local people who were seen as the major beneficiaries of the project. Another trust gave a much larger grant than it had originally intended because it became aware of the tremendously beneficial effects of an early major gift, not only on the cash-flow but also on the credibility of the fundraising campaign and the charity's ability then to ask for other large sums.

Looking to the future

What of the future? To make predictions is to risk becoming a hostage to fortune, but there are some future directions that may tentatively be outlined, based on current trends.

The first is that trusts will tend to become more active in seeking out projects in which they are interested. Some of them will continue a recent trend of becoming fundraisers themselves in order to be able to increase their ability to do what they believe in.

The trusts most likely to increase their giving may well be those that benefit from the increasing profitability of the companies that fund them. With the recent trend of declining interest rates, it might be expected that trusts' ability to grant would be declining (many trusts are governed by the Trustees Investment Act, which restricts the amount of investment they can make in equities and confines them to securer fixed-interest stocks); and yet, on average, this does not seem to be the case. Maybe trusts are bringing some of their capital into play in order to sustain their present level of giving. Maybe founders are putting more money into their trusts to keep up their level of giving. Maybe we have yet to see the true effects of the decline in interest rates. But there does not appear much evidence that the average size of grants is decreasing. Perhaps the picture is obscured by a trend towards giving larger amounts to fewer, better-researched projects.

With regard to what trusts will be seeking to fund in the years ahead, things are unlikely to change very much. Trusts quite often change their policies, but things tend to be cyclical and, as new ideas become old ideas, old ideas come round again as new ones.

Some trusts will continue only to give to capital projects and never to core funding; other trusts will not give to buildings. Many grant-making trusts are most fearful of finding themselves 'on a hook', so to speak, when the charities they support become absolutely dependent upon them. There will always be efforts to wean those charities away from their grant makers.

Grant makers will continue to love pump-priming projects and projects that set a real example to others. Increasingly, they will be looking for serious evaluation of the success or otherwise of the projects that they fund.

A change in wealth creation

Philip Beresford's remarkable research for the *Sunday Times*'s 'Rich List' shows that there is a considerable change in wealth creation in this country. Ten years ago, some 57 per cent of the people on his list had inherited wealth; now fewer than 30 per cent fall into this category – the first time the figure has dropped this low. Yet, people's inherited wealth generally has not suffered in recent years, unless they have, like 'playboys', dissipated it. The reason for the change is the rapid advance of the self-made entrepreneur.

At the same time, it seems that the number of people setting up their own charitable foundations is declining (although the true picture may be clouded by people setting up major CAF Trust Accounts, which are not registered with the Charity Commission and do not therefore become publicly known). Perhaps the greatest challenge for the future will be to promote philanthropy among these people. The ICFM has already started to develop a campaign to do just that.

As times change in future, so, doubtless, will the tasks of grant maker and grant seeker. Major new, and sometimes unexpected, influences will make important differences. We can be rightly apprehensive about stock-market crashes, the effects of inflation, even deflation, new world disasters. But we can be equally optimistic about the arrival on the scene of new super-rich philanthropists, a growing awareness by major companies of the importance of being seen to be providing practical benefits to the community, and of trusts developing new and creative ways of helping good causes with their revenue as well as with their capital-funding needs.

Conclusion

As a final conclusion, here are four key things for you to bear in mind:

- Trusts exist to give money away – if you can prove relevance, they should be truly glad to hear from you.
- Try to ensure that your application is clear and is what the grant maker is looking for.
- Try to arrange things so that your first communication with a trust reaches it through some route other than through the post box – for example, a personal visit, the telephone, a fax or even an e-mail.
- Follow the 10 golden rules listed on the next page, especially the last one. Trusts, like people, do not respond best to requests from institutions, projects, causes or charities. They are happier with requests from people whom they like and respect and who understand their needs.

10 golden rules for approaching trusts

1 Know your charity.
2 Know your trusts.
3 Match your charity to your trusts.
4 Be as personal as possible.
5 Do not send blanket mail shots.
6 Be brief, clear, frank.
7 Avoid jargon, hyperbole, tired words and phrases.
8 Use affirmation – not just assertion.
9 Invest adequately in time and resources.
10 Remember that 'people give to people'.

Glossary of terms used

Accountability The responsibility of a grant-receiving organisation to keep the grant makers informed about the use of the grant.

Acknowledge To express gratitude for (a grant) in written or oral form, communicated privately or publicly.

Action grant A grant awarded to support an operating programme or project (compare research grant).

Administrator The person who administers a grant-making trust.

Advocate To speak or write in favour of a cause, or a person who advocates.

Allocations committee A group responsible for grant-making decisions.

Annual report A yearly report of the financial and overall state of an organisation.

Anonymous gift A gift that is not publicly attributed to the donor.

Appeal letter A letter requesting a donation to a fundraising campaign.

Area of interest A grant-maker's interest in a particular cause.

Benefactor A generous donor.

Bricks/mortar campaign Capital fundraising to meet the financial needs for constructing a building, including fixtures and fittings.

Business plan Specific steps and timetable required to accomplish an organisational objective.

Campaign (fundraising) An organised effort to raise a specified amount of money for a particular purpose in a specified period of time.

Campaign analysis A report on the results and effectiveness of a fundraising campaign.

Capital campaign An intensive fundraising effort to meet a specific financial goal within a specified period of time that is out of the ordinary and not for revenue purposes. Usually for buildings, property, equipment or an endowment.

Capital expenditure The amount needed to acquire an asset having an expected useful life of more than one year.

Case The reason why an organisation both merits and needs philanthropic support.

Case statement A presentation that sets out a case.

Cash flow Funds that are available within a given time.

Cause An ideal or principle served with dedication.

Charitable For or pertaining to charity.

Charitable gift A gift made to a charity.

Charitable trust A trust established to benefit one or more charities.

Charity In the UK this is not fully defined in the law. Generally means an organisation fulfilling charitable purposes (ie the relief of poverty, the advancement of education, the advancement of religion or some other purposed beneficial to the community – the MacNaghten's rules).

Demonstration grant An initial grant given to develop or launch a programme or project that may function as a model.

Direct mail Mass mail sent by an organisation directly to prospects.

Earmark To set aside or designate for a special purpose.

Endowment A permanently restricted net asset, the principle of which is protected and the income from which may be spent on a specific purpose.

Face-to-face Approach in person.

501 (c) (3) US-designated charity, from a section of the Internal Revenue Service Code of the USA.

Foundation Technically a trust whose income derives from an endowment of money or invested capital. In effect synonymous with a 'trust'.

Fundraiser A person, paid or volunteer, who plans, manages or participates in raising funds for an organisation (usually charitable) or cause.

Gift-range table A projection of the number of gifts needed, by size, to achieve a particular fundraising goal.

Grant A financial donation given to support a person, organisation, project or programme of work.

Lead gift A gift donated at the beginning of a campaign that is expected to set a standard for future giving.

Major gift A significant donation, the amount required to qualify as a major gift being determined by the fundraising organisation (usually more than £5,000).

New money A gift of money that exceeds a donor's gift the previous year, or a gift from a newly acquired donor, or a large amount of money recently acquired by a person or family, or self-made rather than inherited wealth.

Old money Wealth inherited by one generation from another.

Overheads General expenses that are necessary to an organisation.

Pledge A promise that is written, signed and dated, to fulfil a commitment at some future time.

Principal A sum of money on which interest is paid.

Prospect Any potential donor whose relationship to the charity, interests and giving ability have been confirmed.

Research grant A grant awarded for scientific or marketing research work.

Settlor Another name for a trustor.

Strategic plan Decisions and action that shape and guide an organisation while emphasising the future implications of present decisions.

Trust An arrangement establishing a judiciary relationship in which a trustor conveys property to a trustee to hold and manage for the benefit of one or more beneficiaries.

Trustee A person or institution holding the legal title to property in a trust and having responsibility for managing it, often a member of a governing board.

Trustor A person making a gift to set up a trust.

Unrestricted gift or grant A gift made without any conditions or designation.

Verbal pledge An oral promise to make a gift or grant.

Working capital Money available to pay current operating expenses.

Useful publications and sources of information

Kay Holmes-Siedle

Charities Aid Foundation (CAF)

The Directory of Grant Making Trusts (DGMT) 1999–2000

Published every other year, currently in its sixteenth edition, containing three volumes. Covers around 3,000 charitable trusts that are cross-referenced under hundreds of fields of charitable interest that they support.

Volume One – The Indices

The trusts that are detailed in Volume One are segregated by:

- beneficial area, ie the geographic area or areas that they prefer to support;
- the specific options, eg the whole of the UK, a specific UK country, a region, a county, a metropolitan area and/or overseas – a trust can therefore appear in up to six lists;
- interest and type of beneficiary, listed according to the type of work a trust is likely to fund in its field of interest, who it wants to benefit and its preferred beneficiaries;
- type of grant.

There is also an index of useful supplies and services.

Comments

The segmentation of information provided in the indices is only one of the tools to use to find out whether a trust is likely to be a potential supporter for your charity. The directory has a number of shortcomings that you should bear in mind when using it:

- It is only produced every two years.
- The indices are a snapshot of one point in time and cannot give a clear indication of whether an area of work is now of major interest for the trust.
- It gives no view of the likely value of grants (past editions of the directory very usefully indicated past grant sizes by a series of numbers).
- It takes no account of the individual interests of the trustees.

- It provides no information on the networks of the trustees. (This may seem unduly unfair: CAF does not claim to provide information on individual trustees, but all good fundraisers know just how important individual trustees can be in influencing a major gift.)
- The religious codes that were a valuable feature of past editions (eg Baptist, Methodist, Jewish, etc) are no longer included.

Volume Two – The Main Register

The main register lists the following core data:

- trust name;
- objects – generally the legal charitable purposes of the trust required for registration at the Charity Commission;
- funding priorities – the main and/or specialist areas of interest of the trust in more detail;
- type of grant – the type of expenditure the trust will support, eg recurrent capital, running costs, etc;
- type of beneficiary – the types of organisation, project or group of people most likely to succeed with an application;
- restrictions – the types of project/cause to which trustees will not make grants;
- beneficial area – the geographical areas where the trust prefers to direct its funding;
- finances – the most up-to-date details available of the trust's income, assets and grants made;
- trustees – list of names and occasionally positions held;
- submission of applications – the trust's rules for the submission of funding requests (including the availability of guidelines) and practice in responding to applications;
- correspondent – the name and address of the person (or company) to whom correspondence relating to the activities of the trust should be directed;
- Charity Commission number;
- established – the year of the trust's foundation.

Comments

- This is good basic information that should begin to allow you to make some early judgements on whether the trust is worth considering.
- The information needs to be updated from other sources on a regular basis, eg the trust may be too small, or you may now need to find out much more about the trust policy, past grants and its trustees.

Provides individual entries for the major grant-making trusts (ranked according to their position in 'CAF's top 500 grant-making trusts' in the 1998 edition of *Dimensions of the Voluntary Sector*). The following data is listed:

- the trust's name
- its funding priorities
- what it does not fund
- who can qualify for grants
- types of grant typically given
- type of expenditure trusts will support
- range of grants given
- list of trustees
- how to apply and whom to apply to.

Trust Watch

This is a quarterly newsletter that is sent, free of charge, to all purchasers of the *DGMT* and *Grantseeker* CD-ROM (see below). Its aim is to keep readers up to date with news about what is happening in the field of charitable trusts and foundations. The first issue includes:

- information on new trusts not published in the current edition of the *DGMT* or *Grantseeker* (the CD-ROM);
- features on the new foundations being set up by building societies;
- an article on the New Opportunities Fund, the National Lottery's sixth good cause, as well as other Lottery news;
- latest developments in some of the major trusts;
- new developments in the field of charitable trusts and foundations.

The DGMT Focus series

This series includes the following titles:

Children and Youth (1998)

Focuses on trusts supporting causes in the field of work.

Environment, Animal Welfare and Heritage
International
Museum, Galleries and the Performing Arts
Religion (second edition)
Schools, Colleges and Educational Establishments
Social Care
Trustees Index (new edition in 2000)
An alphabetical list of the trustees whose names are in the *DGMT*.

Grantseeker (1999–2000)

An interactive CD-ROM designed to scan the entire *DGMT* database and to provide users with a 'hit-list' of trusts whose funding preferences match their project or cause. Renewed every six months, and available on a subscription basis.

The Directory of Social Change (DSC)

A Guide to the Major Trusts Vol 1

Published every other year; covers 300 trusts that make grants of over £200,000 a year and gives examples of actual grants they have made.

A Guide to the Major Trusts Vol 2

Published every other year as above; covers 700 trusts that make grants of at least £50,000 a year.

These volumes provide not only factual and publicly available information on name, grants budget, objects, address, telephone number, contact, names, trustee examples of grants, exclusions and application details but also independent commentary on the work of some of the grant-making trusts.

The following trusts are generally excluded:

- company charitable trusts;
- single issue trusts;
- those funding only overseas activities;
- public purse grant makers;
- smaller local trusts;
- those supporting only a narrow range of medical research.

Trust profiles are shown alphabetically, with indices by funding size, subject and geographical classification with the warning that the indices should only be used as a tool for helping you locate your best prospects, not for providing a definitive list.

Comments

These books are excellent. However, because they provide such a proliferation of information, do not be lured into believing that your work is done for you. A good trust fundraiser should, for a major prospect, look at the activities of a trust over a 2–3-year period so as to be clear about its future intent and have some good solid information on the trustees, their backgrounds, networks and likely motivations.

Trust Monitor

A journal published three times a year (in March, July and November) covering:

- news/comment on existing trust activities;
- news on establishment of, or rumoured, new trusts;
- in-depth interviews with trust administrators and directors;
- update on new trust addresses;
- policy changes in the top 400 trusts;
- mini-profiles of new trusts and trusts previously unlisted in any publication, together with new activity information on well-established trusts.

Comments

A good, cheap and unmissable update service.

The Scottish Trusts Guide (1996)

A new publication providing a guide to grant-making trusts that are based in Scotland or that give priority to applications from Scottish groups. Covers about 350 trusts which together give over £40 million a year to voluntary organisations in Scotland. Many trusts in this publication appear in print for the first time.

Writing Better Fundraising Applications

Michael Norton and Michael Eastwood (2nd edition, published in association with ICFM).

Comments

This is an excellent resource that every trust fundraiser should have in their office, but it is not intended to be an exhaustive guide.

EUROPA

International Foundation Directory (1998)

This publication states that, to qualify for entry, each trust must have:

- objects, recognised as charitable or for the public benefit;
- substantial assets, establishing it as a permanent institution;
- discretion in the allocation of its money, thus excluding those specifically set up to fund a particular cause (eg a named school or hospital) or as a smaller part of another institution that would be listed in its own right;
- operate internationally in some way, primarily through grants or the impact of their programmes (ie not all trusts listed are grant givers).

Most entries contain the establishment's name, address, telephone, e-mail (and fax numbers) and their Internet address, as well as the date of foundation, their primary aims, activities, finances, publications and key executives.

The publication also contains an alphabetical list of foundations, an index of main activities and a brief paper on the history of foundations in different countries and their future role for the next century.

Comments

An ambitious directory, surveying trusts and foundations in 108 countries, this is, for many charities operating globally, an essential source. Its editor, Cathy Hartley, faces a more than usually hard task of locating and updating well over 1,000 entries. The book's sources are:

- revised updates of earlier entries provided by individual trusts or foundations;
- secondary publications;
- other international foundation centres;
- the Internet.

If a trust/foundation fails or refuses to provide up-to-date information, the publishers do not undertake desk research. That explains, for example, why some UK entries do not contain the latest Charity Commission information.

Where a country has many trusts operating internationally (eg the UK and USA), the editor has selected these trusts with the greatest assets, income or grants or those that have demonstrated a significant activity or support outside their own country.

The directory has improved with each publication. The editor hopes, even allowing for the language difficulty and inexactitude of the Internet search drivers, to continue to locate new trusts.

RTI Publications

Funding Digest

Subscription based, this publication offers a monthly information service for voluntary and public-sector organisations. Available in paper form or in electronic format (disk or e-mail) for multiple users. Single-user subscriptions are available only to smaller, local voluntary organisations and charities for their own internal fundraising use; multiple-user subscriptions carry an additional cost and are intended for larger organisations.

Comments

This provide welcome up-to-date information on some new trusts and the changing policies and interests of some established trusts. It will often provide two or three in-depth pages of information on the policy and grants activities of a specific trust.

- Good and ongoing coverage of the numerous and complicated activities of the European Funds.
- A section covering the gossip, activities and deadlines for the various Lottery boards.

In July 1998 the publishers launched Fdonline – a website giving faster access to information, access to past linked information and more detailed information that appears in the paper version, and links to other useful information sites.

The Factary

New Trust Update

A limited-edition subscription service, this provides a monthly report on approximately 20 newly registered trusts. Information includes name, registration number, address, telephone number, contact name, objects, area of benefit, income (often unknown at this early date), trustees' names and addresses and researchers' comments. Here are two examples of a trust's entry:

> This is a new trust and is still awaiting funds. The correspondent suggested that interested charities contact him in about six months' time for further details.

> This company is providing financial services and has been involved with charitable causes for some time – debt counselling was one of those mentioned.

Comments

- It's always good to be spotting early opportunities, but remember the generosity and scope of many of the trusts will often not be known in the first year.
- Almost certainly worth subscribing to and monitoring its effectiveness as a source of new funds.

The Foundation Center

The Foundation Center publishes a number of useful publications for US foundation grant-seekers, among which are:

The Foundation Directory
The Foundation 1,000 (1997–98)
Guide to US Foundations

Fundraising Research & Consultancy Ltd

Donor Digest

A weekly digest of useful information gathered over the previous seven days from the *Financial Times, Daily Telegraph, Guardian, Independent, Sunday Times, Observer, Independent on Sunday, Sunday Telegraph, Daily Mail, Business Age, Tatler, Hello, Sponsorship News* and *Marketing Week.*

The publication includes up-to-the minute details on the establishment of new trusts, particularly those where the very rich are establishing a foundation for their personal gifts. Here is an example of an entry:

> Hugh Stevenson, MAMS Chairman received an estimated £24 million when the company was taken over. He said £9.26 million of the money he received was destined for a Charitable Trust..... *Times*, 15 June 1998.

Comments

The many individual profiles will provide essential information on the lives, interests and motivations of many UK trustees.

The Association of Community Trusts and Foundations (ACTAF)

This is a first point of reference for understanding who and where community trusts and foundations are based. Each one is of course concerned with a specific geographic area and will not normally have grant-making income to support any work outside its area.

ACTAF has 19 full members and 29 associates.

At the end of March 1997, 18 community foundations had given over £9.8 million in grants in the previous year.

Comments

Researchers need to locate which geographic areas are relevant to their charities before requesting specific annual reports and trust objectives from each specific foundation.

The Charity Commission

All researchers must become well acquainted with the database and trusts' paper files available from the London or regional offices of the Charity Commission, or via the Internet.

Comments

Although it can frequently be time consuming and frustrating, there can be real value in looking at a trust's paper files, particularly to see:

- the names and addresses of the original trustees;
- how and why the trust came into being;
- new trustee information if the names have changed;
- past grants list (the last 2–3 years can often give you a very good idea of the priorities and motivations of the trustees – this information should be used to supplement the 'snapshot' one-year information that published sources often provide).

The Charity Commission may be the only source of information about some of the special trusts on a charity's donor database.

Caritas Data

Top 1000 Charities in Scotland

This book provides information on the voluntary sector in Scotland, currently estimated at £1.5 billion. The information is principally provided for the benefit of fundraisers, grant makers and corporate donors, charity executives, researchers and marketing professionals.

- Gives details on top 1000 charities in Scotland.
- Identifies the people behind the top charities
- Locates professional advisors.
- Presents contact details of a further 22,000 charities.
- Uses league tables to enable comparison of charities' performance.

Chapel & York

Supply a very useful range of publications about USA grant-making foundations, among which are the following:

Complete Guide to the Top US International Foundation Grantmakers
Fundraising from America

CD-Roms and disks – electronically based reference systems

There are two main trust CD-ROMs available. They are provided by CAF and the DSC.

A diskette is also provided by Funder Finder, which has been much involved with the production of the DSC's CD-ROM.

All will provide a prospect list of trusts after selection criteria has been entered.

The ability of these sources to provide an authoritative list hinges on three key factors:

- the quality, depth and accuracy of the original trust information;
- how the above information is coded by the information provider;
- the sophistication of the system's search drivers.

Comments

These relatively new devices have been variously reviewed. In theory they represent an enormous advance in fundraisers' ability to track down suitable trust sources. Unfortunately, they can be as misleading as they can be helpful. For example, a test selection was undertaken against each of these three electronic sources, with specific search criteria. Each database came up with very different results. The results were then compared with the research undertaken using personal knowledge, a fundraising consultancy's internal database and validating telephone calls with the trusts themselves. Of the 20 trusts on the final list (most of which had, in the course of the telephone calls, confirmed that they had an interest in the project) no fewer than 12 failed to appear on the electronically generated lists.

Researchers therefore need to be very careful in their use of these sources. Undoubtedly, they can be a useful tool in helping in the early selection of a prospect trust list, but they are not yet ready to replace knowledgeable, manual research.

Regional and local guides

The following are some useful regional and local publications from the above, and other, publishing sources:

- East Midlands: *The Directory of Grant Making Trusts, Focus Series: Cambridgeshire, Norfolk and the East Midlands* (CAF)
- London: *A Guide to Local Trusts in Greater London 1996–97* (DSC)
- Merseyside: *Merseyside Directory of Grant Making Trusts 1993–94* (Communications Department, Liverpool CVS, 14 Castle St, Liverpool, L2 0NJ)
- Midlands: *A Guide to Local Trusts in the Midlands 1996–97* (DSC)

- North: *A Guide to Local Trusts in the North of England 1996–97* (DSC)
- North East: *The North-East Guide for Grant Seekers 1996–97* and *The North-East Guide for Grants to Individuals* (Funding Information North East, John Haswell House, 8–9 Gladstone Terrace, Gateshead, NE8 4DY
  The Directory of Grant Making Trusts, Focus Series: Yorkshire, Humberside and the North East (CAF)
- North West: *The Directory of Grant Making Trusts, Focus Series: Manchester, Liverpool and the North West* (CAF)
- Northern Ireland: *Funding for Voluntary Action – A Guide to Local Trusts in Northern Ireland 1995–96* (Northern Ireland Voluntary Trust, 22 Mount Charles, Belfast, BT7 1NZ)
- Scotland: *Directory of Scottish Grant Making Trusts* (Scottish Council for Voluntary Organisations, 18–19 Claremont Crescent, Edinburgh EH7 4QD)
  The Scottish Trusts Guide (DSC)
- South: *A Guide to Local Trusts in the South of England 1996–97* (DSC)
- Wales: *Wales Funding Handbook* (Wales Council for Voluntary Action, Crescent Road, Caerphilly CF8 1XL).

Grants in specialist fields

- The DSC publishes a series of specialist guides, such as the *Arts Funding Guide 1997–98, Peace and International Relations, Sports Funding Guide 1996–97*, and others. Ask for their booklist. Where no specialist guide exists, the only sources of information are the generalist guides.
- CAF also publishes some specialist guides (eg *Environment, Animal Welfare and Heritage, Children and Youth, International*) as part of the *Directory of Grant Making Trusts Focus* series: these guides carry no information beyond that in the *Directory of Grant Making Trusts*.

Government grant and corporate giving

- See these DSC publications: *A Guide to UK Company Giving, The Guide to Funding from Government Departments and Agencies 1998)*.

International funders

- *Third World Directory 1997–98* (published by the DSC) gives details of over 200 organisations based in the UK and working in the developing world and Eastern Europe (very few UK grant-making trusts fund outside the UK; most of those that do are listed in this book).
- *International Foundation Directory 1996* (published by Europa Publications, 18 Bedford Square, London WC1B 3JN) gives details of 1,200 foundations and other bodies that fund internationally.

- *US Foundation Support in Europe 1994* (published by the DSC).
- *Directory of Foundation and Corporate Members of the European Foundation Centre* (published by the European Foundation Centre, 51 rue de la Concorde, B–1050 Brussels, Belgium; tel: +32 2 512 .89 38 Fax: +32.2. 512 32 65).
- *International Guide to Funders Interested in Eastern and Central Europe* (published by the European Foundation Centre – details as above).
- *UK Charitable Funding for the Republic of Ireland 1995* (published by the DSC).

Funds for individuals

- *A Guide to Grants for Individuals in Need 1998–99* (published by the DSC) provides information on 2,100 service and ex-service charities, trade union welfare funds, occupational benevolent funds, disability charities, local and parochial and national charities – all of which give financial support to individuals and a yearly total of £150 million.
- *Charities Digest 2000* (Waterlows Information Services Ltd, Paulton House, 8 Shepherdess Walk, London N1 7LB; tel 020 7490 0049) gives details of 1,200 national and regional charities, many of which give grants to individuals. It also contains complete lists of local advisory bodies such as citizens advice bureaux and law centres (which will advise individuals in need), councils for voluntary service, rural community councils, and federations of community.

Useful Internet addresses

Association of Charitable Foundations http://www.acf.org.uk/foundations
Charitable Trusts Information http://www.york.ac.uk/admin/ido/charitie.htm
Charities Aid Foundation – details on 70,000 charities http://www.charitynet.org
Charity Commission, Central Register http://www.open.gov.uk/charity/ccintro.htm
Council of Foundations http://www.cof.org
The Council of Foundations (USA) http://www.picnet.com/cof
The Foundation Center on-line http://fdncenter.org/
Philanthropy journal on line http://www.philanthropy-journal.org/
UK fundraising resource site for non-profits http://www.fundraising.co.uk
Other charity websites http://pitch.phon.ucl.ac.uk/home/dave/TOCH/Charities/

Useful organisations (including training providers)

The American Fund for Charities
c/o Chapel & York Limited
1215 17th Street NW
Washington DC 20036
USA

The American Fund for Charities (UK address)
c/o Chapel & York Limited
PO Box 50
Lingfield
RH7 6FT
UK
tel: 01342 836790

Association of Charitable Foundations (ACF)
4 Bloomsbury Square
London
WC1A 2RL
tel: 020 7404 1338

Association of Community Trusts and Foundations (ACTAF)
4 Bloomsbury Square
London
WC1A 2RL
tel: 020 7831 0033

Umbrella organisation which all community trusts and foundations in the UK belong to.

British Schools and Universities Foundation
575 Madison Avenue
Suite 1006
New York
New York 10022–2511.
tel: 212 662 5576.

Caritas Data

Kemp House
152–160 City Road
London
EC1V 2NP
tel: 020 7250 1777

Chapel & York Ltd

P O Box 50
Lingfield
RH7 6FT
tel: 01342 836790

A company that specialises in helping UK charities to seek grants from US foundations.

Charity Commission

Harmonsworth House
13–15 Bouverie Street
London
EC4Y 8DP
tel: 0870 333 0123

2nd Floor
20 Kings Parade
Queen's Dock
Liverpool
L3 4DQ
tel: 0870 333 0123

Woodfield House
Tangier
Taunton
Somerset
TA1 4BL
tel: 0870 333 0123

Charities Aid Foundation (CAF)

Kings Hill
West Malling
Kent
ME19 4TA
tel: 01732 520000

Charities Aid Foundation America

King Street Station
Suite 150
1800 Diagonal Road
Alexandria
Virginia 22314
USA
tel: 703 549 8931

Directory of Social Change

24 Stephenson Way
London
NW1 2DP
tel: 020 7209 4949

An educational charity that publishes a wide range of books designed to help charities to raise funds from a number of different sources. The DSC also runs training workshops and seminars throughout the UK. Two such courses are:

- *Raising Money from Trusts* – 1-day course, Level 1; £85–£120
  This one-day course looks at the different types of charitable trust, how and why they give support and how best to apply for it.
- *Charitable Trusts, developing and Increasing Your Support* – 1-day course, Level 2; £85–£125
  This follow-on course from *Raising Money from Trusts* is aimed at those organisations that already receive support from trusts and foundations and will discuss ways to develop and increase that support.

Directory of Trustees

6 Stoneleigh Crescent
Ewell
Surrey
KT19 0RP
tel: 020 8393 3885

Provides an alphabetical listing of the names of trustees with the names and addresses of their trusts.

The Factary

The Coach House
Upper York Street
Bristol
BS2 8QN
tel: 0117 924 0663

Provides a research service for fundraisers and organisations.

The Foundation Center
79 Fifth Avenue
New York
NY 10003–3076
tel: 212 620 4230
fax: 212 807 3677
Web address: www.fdncenter.org

Fresh Fields Training
The Little House
Bath Road
Norton St Phillip
Bath
BA3 6LP
tel: 01373 834497

Although the organisation offers nothing specifically on trust fundraising, the subject is included in their general fundraising course.

Funder Finder
Funder Finder
65 Raglan Road
Leeds
LS2 9DZ
tel: 0113 242 3008

Produces computer software for grant seekers that is designed to help them identify the trusts most likely to help them – many local CVSs have access to this system so you might try them in the first instance (see NACVS on the next page).

FR&C LTD (Fundraising Research and Consultancy Ltd)
Tebbit House
Winchcombe Street
Cheltenham
GL52 2NE
tel: 0124 252 2323

Provides a research and consultancy service based on a database and press-cutting library holding over 40,000 records of companies, trusts and individuals. Publishes a weekly *Donor Digest* of information about individuals and corporate targeting.

Institute of Charity Fundraising Managers (ICFM)

5th floor
Market Towers
1 Nine Elms Lane
London
SW8 5NQ
tel: 020 7627 3436

The professional body for charity fundraisers in the UK. Publishes a range of information, including monthly update service for members and *Who's Who in Fundraising*, an annual yearbook. Also offers a wide range of training programmes in all aspects of fundraising practice to those just starting out and to the more seasoned professional. The Certificate in Fundraising Management is the Institute's professional qualification for all fundraisers.

ICFM Training offers a one-day course on *Fundraising from Grant-Making Trusts and Foundations*, costing £170–£200, which provides participants with detailed knowledge and background information on the trust environment, how to plan and execute targeted approaches to grant-making bodies and how to develop continuing and fruitful relationships with them. ICFM staff trainers are skilled in learning-process design, hold professional training qualifications and are members of the Institute of Personnel and Development.

London Voluntary Services Council

356 Holloway Road
London
N7 6PA
tel: 020 7700 8107

Runs seminars and workshops and publishes *Voluntary Voice*, a magazine that appears ten times a year.

National Association of Councils for Voluntary Service (NACVS)

3rd Floor
Arundel Court
177 Arundel Street
Sheffield
S2 2NU
tel: 0114 278 6636

Umbrella organisation for local Councils for Voluntary Service (CVS). Will advise you of your nearest CVS and will also give information of training possibilities in your area.

National Council for Voluntary Organisations (NCVO)
Regent's Wharf
8 All Saints Street
London
N1 9RL
tel: 020 7713 6161

An umbrella body offering help and advice (especially legal advice) to all charitable organisations.

London Voluntary Service Council
356 Holloway Road
London
N7 6PA
tel: 020 7700 8107

This council offers nothing specifically on trusts, but there is a one-day course that combines fundraising from trusts and fundraising from companies.

The Management Centre
336 Kennington Road
London
SE11 4DB
tel: 020 7820 1100

There is no permanent trust course on the Centre's prospectus, but it may do a one-day course at some point in the future.

The Projects Company
tel: 020 8502 2327

Prospecting for Gold (also known as Charity Consultants)
Little Holme
Station Road
Shiplake
Henley on Thames
Oxon
RG9 3JS
tel: 0118 940 1016

Offers a four-day course on *Developing Trust Fundraising Skills*, costing £525 (+VAT), which provides an in-depth look at ways to improve your application techniques to grant-making trusts. At the end of the course, which is taken in two parts, participants will have improved their research skills and will be better able to create a strategy to achieve targeted income from trusts, present their work effectively and devise different means of approach to suit different situations.

K G Saur

Ortlerstrasse 8
D-81373 Munich
Germany
tel: 49 89 769020

Scottish Council for Voluntary Organisations (SCVO)

18–19 Claremont Crescent
Edinburgh
EH7 4QD
The Scottish equivalent of the NCVO.

References

Booth and Mullin R (1976) *Report on Foundation Activity*. West Malling: CAF.

Debrett's Peerage (1999) *Debrett's People of Today*. London: Debrett's Peerage Ltd.

Pharoah C and Siederer N (1997) 'Numbers, income, grants and assets – new estimates' in Pharoah C (ed) *Dimensions of the Voluntary Sector*. West Malling: CAF.

Pharoah C (1997) 'Interests, activities and policies of grant-makers – new data' in Pharoah C (ed) (1997) *Dimensions of the Voluntary Sector*. West Malling: CAF.

Rattigan A (ed) (1997) *Baring Asset Management Top 3000 Charities*. London: Caritas Data Ltd.

Villemur A (1996) *Applying to a Grant Making Trust: a guide for fundraisers*. West Malling: CAF.

About CAF

CAF, Charities Aid Foundation, is a registered charity with a unique mission – to increase the substance of charity in the UK and overseas. It provides services that are both charitable and financial which help donors make the most of their giving and charities make the most of their resources.

Many of CAF's publications reflect the organisation's purpose: *Dimensions of the Voluntary Sector* offers the definitive financial overview of the UK voluntary sector, while the *Directory of Grant Making Trusts* provides the most comprehensive source of funding information available.

As an integral part of its activities, CAF works to raise standards of management in voluntary organisations. This includes the making of grants by its own Grants Council, sponsorship of the Charity Annual Report and Accounts Awards, seminars, training courses and the Charities Annual Conference, the largest regular gathering of key people from within the voluntary sector. In addition, Charitynet (www.charitynet.org) is now established as the leading Internet site on voluntary action.

For decades, CAF has led the way in developing tax-effective services to donors, and these are now used by more than 250,000 individuals and 2,000 of the UK's leading companies, between them giving £150 million each year to charity. Many are also using CAF's CharityCard, the world's first debit card designed exclusively for charitable giving. CAF's unique range of investment and administration services for charities includes the CafCash High Interest Cheque Account, two common investment funds for longer-term investment and a full appeals and subscription management service.

CAF's activities are not limited to the UK, however. Increasingly, CAF is looking to apply the same principles and develop similar services internationally, in its drive to increase the substance of charity across the world. CAF has offices and sister organisations in the United States, Bulgaria, South Africa, Russia, India and Brussels.

For more information about CAF, please visit www.CAFonline.org/

Other publications from CAF

The Directory of Grant Making Trusts

16th Edition
ISBN 1–85934–078–4   £89.95 (3 Volumes)

Grant making trusts represent a major source of support for charitable activity in the UK – in 1997 alone they contributed over £1.9 billion.

Grant making trusts support a wide variety of causes and their criteria for allocating funds are often very specific. The *Directory of Grant Making Trusts* (*DGMT*) keeps fundraisers in touch with changes in trusts' funding priorities. Its extensive indexing allows great precision in the targeting of trusts – thus reducing the flow of irrelevant applications and saving time and money at both ends.

The information published in the *DGMT* is the result of extensive research and close liaison with the trust community; it provides the most comprehensive picture of UK trusts currently published. As well as listing over 3,500 trusts – of which 1,500 are new to this edition – the directory now features top 10 sample grants for hundreds of trusts and a new index by grant type. With the addition of the new third volume providing detailed commentaries on 250 of the major trusts, the *DGMT* now represents a complete, one-stop information shop for the trust fundraiser.

Grantseeker

The interactive CD-ROM for fundraisers
£58.69 (incl VAT) for each six-monthly release

Drawing on CAF's years of experience as a publisher of the *Directory of Grant Making Trusts*, *Grantseeker* is the tailor-made solution to the information needs of trust fundraisers in the electronic age. Published for the first time as a subscription service, users will receive a completely new updated edition every six months.

Fully interactive, *Grantseeker*'s specially designed search engine will quickly scan the entire DGMT database on the basis of a user's own selection criteria and generate a 'hit list' of trusts whose funding preferences match their project or cause. There are two additional search functions: the ability to search on trustees' names and a key word search by town or city which allows users a more closely defined geographical search. Users' bookmarks and notes automatically carry over to each new release.

Taking full advantage of the extra options available via an electronic search tool, *Grantseeker* offers a more sophisticated matching service than can be provided by traditional methods, enabling fundraisers to save weeks of effort and frustration. A simple hypertext link can provide them with a complete DGMT entry on a potential funder within moments of loading the CD. The days of ultimate dependence on a paper-based directory are over.

Grantseeker runs under Windows 95 or above.

The CAF/ICFM Fundraising Series

Corporate Fundraising

Valerie Morton (editor)
ISBN 1–85934–057–1   £19.95

Corporate Fundraising offers a comprehensive overview of its subject, detailing the variety of ways in which charities and companies may work together to mutual advantage. The book presents a structured approach to this branch of fundraising, demonstrating how detailed research, nurturing individual contacts and carefully planning the formal approach may significantly enhance the possibility of success.

Fundraising Strategy

Redmond Mullin
ISBN 1-85934-056-3   £14.95

Fundraising today demands a substantial commitment of people, resources and marketing. Rigorous, strategic planning is a prerequisite if a campaign is to achieve success and a viable return on investment. This book aims to clarify the principle and process of strategy and to demonstrate its place in fundraising campaigns.

Legacy Fundraising

Sebastian Wilberforce
ISBN 1-85934-055-5   £14.95

Legacy fundraising is a specialist activity. Charities need to recognise its unique characteristics and sensitivities and devise a strategy based on detailed research into past and future supporters. The contributors to this book demonstrate the formulation of such an approach in practice, mixing practical case histories with more theoretical exposition.

About the ICFM

The ICFM was established in 1983 to provide an individual membership body committed to the highest standards in fundraising for not-for-profit organisations and charities. The Institute now has over 3,000 individual members working in or for charities and voluntary organisations in a fundraising capacity. In addition, the Institute's Charitable Trust has over 400 national, regional and local charities and companies affiliated to its aims and objectives.

All members of the Institute agree, as a point of membership, to abide by its Code of Conduct and various Codes of Practice and Guidance Notes. The Institute administers a structured three-tier training programme covering all aspects of fundraising technique and management. Individual members of the Institute receive the *Update* newsletter, keeping them abreast of changes in work practice and amendments to law at national and international level. Through its eleven regional groups, individual members of the Institute have the opportunity to meet other fundraisers operating in their own locality, to discuss issues of common concern and to participate in training programmes and in the policy development of the ICFM as a whole.

Each year the Institute manages the National Fundraising Convention, the major annual focus for fundraising activity in the United Kingdom, held over three days in the Birmingham area.

The ICFM is recognised by government, the Charity Commission and, increasingly, throughout the voluntary sector as the lead body in providing self-regulation in fundraising practice. This process is managed through compliance with the Code of Conduct and through the development of a range of Codes of Practice covering specific fundraising techniques and designed to provide clear guidance to practising fundraisers on what is efficient, effective and, above all, appropriate practice.

The ICFM promotes research into existing and developing fundraising techniques, and provides a central base for information and data on fundraising held in its library at its national offices in London.

Any individual or charity actively fundraising is eligible to apply for either individual membership or corporate affiliation of the ICFM.

Other publications from the ICFM

Published codes of practice

	Member	Non-member
Code of Practice on Reciprocal Mailing	£1.25	£2.50
Code of Practice on Schools	£1.25	£2.50
Code of Practice on Telephone Recruitment of Collectors	£1.25	£2.50
The Scottish Code of Fundraising Practice	£5.00	£10.00
The Use of Chain Letters	£1.25	£2.50
Static Collection Boxes	£1.25	£2.50
Outbound Telephone Support	£1.25	£2.50
House to House Collections	£1.25	£2.50
Acceptance/Refusal of Donations	£1.25	£2.50
Code of Practice on Outdooor Events	£1.25	£2.50
Consultants Group Code of Practice	FREE	FREE
Code of Practice on Legacies	£1.25	£2.50

Published books

	Member	Non-member
The Complete Fundraising Handbook *Sam Clark*	£13.95	£14.95
Charity Appeals: the complete guide to success *Marion Allford*	£13.59	£15.99
Writing Better Fundraising Applications *Michael Norton*	£9.95	£12.95
Who's Who in Fundraising	£10.00	£20.00
Schools Fundraising *Ann Mountfield*	£10.50	£12.95
Fundraising on the Internet *Howard Lake*	£10.50	£12.95
Handbook of Fundraising Consultancy	£6.00	£12.00
Reference Manual on Payroll Giving	FREE	£2.50

To order any of the above publications, please contact:

ICFM, Central Office, Market Towers, 1 Nine Elms Lane, London SW8 5NQ
Telephone 020 7627 3436/020 7978 2761

Index